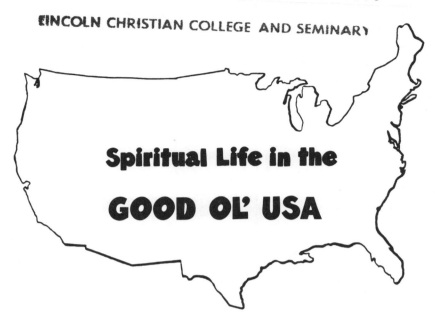

Spiritual Life in the

GOOD OL' USA

Story-Essays

on Popular Culture and Christianity

Melvin Hasman

The
Potter's
Books

La Mesa, California   •   Mansfield, Ohio

Copyright © 1994 by Melvin D. Hasman
Printed in the United States of America

First printing 1994
1   2   3   4   5   6   7   8   9—99   98   97   96   95   94

Library of Congress Cataloging in Publication Data

Hasman, Melvin, 1938–
    Spiritual life in the Good Ol' USA : story-essays on popular
culture and Christianity / Melvin Hasman.
        p.   cm.
    ISBN 0-9638240-8-2 (alk. paper) : $23.95. — ISBN 0-9638240-9-0
(pbk. : alk. paper) : $15.95
    1. Popular culture—Religious aspects—Christianity.   2. Popular
culture—United States.   3. Christian life—1960–   I. Title.
BR115.C8H387   1994
261'.0973—dc20   93-34388
                                                           CIP

BIBLE TRANSLATIONS

NIV—Scripture taken from the HOLY BIBLE, NEW INTERNATIONAL
    VERSION. NIV. Copyright © 1973, 1978, 1984 by International Bible
    Society. Used by permission of Zondervan Publishing House. All rights
    reserved.
Amplified—From The Amplified Bible, Old Testament. Copyright © 1965,
    1987 by The Zondervan Corporation. The Amplified New Testament,
    copyright © 1954, 1958, 1987 by The Lockman Foundation. Used by
    permission.
RSV (and the New RSV)—*The Holy Bible Revised Standard Version.*
Phillips—*The New Testament in Modern English.*
KJV (and the New KJV)—*The Holy Bible King James Version.*
Smith-Goodspeed—*The Complete Bible: An American Translation.*
NAS—*Holy Bible New American Standard.*

The
Potter's
Books

Office PO Box 2133   *Orders* 1444 US Rt. 42, RD 11
        La Mesa CA 91943-2133   Mansfield, OH 44903
                                                  TEL 800/247-6553
                                                  FAX 419/281-6883

Preface

The Writing of *Spiritual Life in the Good Ol' USA*

Here is a behind the scenes look at some of the story-essays in the collection.

The Scarecrow and the Wizard of Schools

Nine judges ruling a nation is maddening. Even worse is watching 250,000,000 Munchkins trembling with fear. The idea was to write something simple and with a light touch that Munchkins could understand. Then it was simply a matter of stripping the chief justice of his booming voice, black robe, and showing him to be just another emperor with no clothes.

Alice in . . . (*Censored!*)

It is a short journey from Oz to Wonderland. I needed a naive youth to wander into the dark world where caterpillars (artists beyond the fringe) create their art.

94954

Me, Jane

It was Christmas morning. I awoke and in my mind's eye saw a setting of the Garden of Eden, with Eve running from it. Looking more closely at the setting, it became a jungle where Tarzan and Jane lived. Different as these two settings were, I saw them as one.

Hurrying out of bed, I began writing. As I wrote that Christmas morning, I felt the story was a gift from Jesus—now the exalted son—to his mother, Mary, who did not run from God. In my mind's eye, I saw Mary, a small person in the picture. With a simple gesture toward the earth, she smiled and offered the story-gift to women on earth.

Civil War

If only someone could wave a wand of legislation and bring goodwill to the hearts of people. On this dream marches civil rights. It cannot be. The deeper matter of the heart is dealt with in this war story, a story of how a stone wall separating brothers can be taken down stone by stone.

The Stork Knows the Season

Every story-essay in this book has been critiqued by eight professional writers. We have been meeting monthly for 17 years. Said one writer of the "Stork": "Parts read like poetry." Said another, "It's good. But what use is it?"

What use was it for a psalmist to look into the heavens? Perhaps just to feel small before majesty.

Directive: Spiritual Gifts Are *Not* for Today

I grew up methodically—as a Methodist. As a baby, I was baptized. As a child, I was promoted through the Sunday School. As a youth, I was ushered into membership on Palm Sunday. As a young man, I was given the seal of approval as the bishop laid hands on me.

Yet in my progress as a Methodist pilgrim, I kept looking around for where Jesus Christ was. It seems I always suspected that the church—the Organization—had replaced the Christ.

Said most of my critique group: "We love the cleverness, but what you say INFURIATES us!" Through 15 blistering minutes, I kept telling myself, "These are my friends. These are my friends. These are my friends. . ."

The House Painter's Ladder

I may be the only one who thinks this is the best story-essay of the lot, but as the years pass by, I think the ladder will rise high above the others.

Contents

List of Illustrations

Paintings

Guernica by Pablo Picasso, © 1992 ARS, New York/SPADEM, Paris. Page 75.

The Sacrament of the Last Supper by Salvador Dali. Chester Dale Collection, © 1993 National Gallery of Art, Washington. Page 90.

Christ Mocked by Soldiers by Georges Rouault. (1932) Oil on canvas, 36 1/4 × 28 1/2″. Collection, The Museum of Modern Art, New York. Given anonymously. Page 92.

Animals in a Landscape (Painting with Bulls II) by Franz Marc. © The Detroit Institute of Arts. Gift of Robert H. Tannahill. Page 94.

Editorial Cartoons

HERE COMES MY DAD by Jack Gold. Reprinted courtesy of *The Kentucky Post*. Page 19.

OH, COME ON! by Steve Kelley. *San Diego Union*. Used by permission of Copley News Service and Steve Kelley. Page 21.

SEE JOHNNY by Mike Ramirez. *Memphis Commercial Appeal*. Reprinted by permission: Michael P. Ramirez, *The Commercial Appeal*/Copley News Service. Page 23.

WE'LL BE ALRIGHT by Bob Murphy. *Manchester Union-Leader*. Page 47.

THE PILGRIMS CAME by Wayne Stayskal. *Tampa Tribune*. Reprinted by permission: Tribune Media Services. Page 52.

MR. HILL, MY SON by Chuck Asay. Reprinted by permission of the *Colorado Springs Sun*. Page 53.

YES, HE'S DEFINITELY PRAYING by David Horsey. Reprinted courtesy of the *Seattle Post-Intelligencer*. Page 56.

BY A VOTE OF 7 TO 2 by Wayne Stayskal. © copyrighted 1983, Chicago Tribune Company, all rights reserved, used with permission. Page 57.

THE GREAT AMERICAN BABY-SITTER by Bob Palmer. *Springfield (MO) Leader-Press*. Reprinted courtesy of Bob Palmer. Page 70.

DEATH OF A SALESMAN by Bob Sullivan. Reprinted from the *Worcester Telegram*. Cartoon by Bob Sullivan, 1974. Page 106.

SO WHAT IF I HAVE by Wayne Stayskal. *Chicago Today*. Reprinted by permission: Tribune Media Services. Page 114.

CULTS by Ed Fischer. Reprinted courtesy of *The Omaha World-Herald*. Page 182.

Drawings

Illustrations from the land of Oz (but not the Witch) are the originals drawn by W. W. Denslow for L. Frank Baum's *The Wizard of Oz*. The Scarecrow and Toto each holding a sheet of paper are composites.

The illustration of Alice is a detail from the original drawing by John Tenniel for Lewis Carroll's *Alice's Adventures in Wonderland*.

The cover, designed by the author, uses mostly clip art.
The author's photo is by Photographic Images By Faith.

Don't allow yourself
to be overpowered with evil.
Take the offensive—
     overpower evil by good!
          —Romans 12:21 Phillips

Dorothy Meets the Witch
of Government Schools

IT WAS a summer's day in Kansas.[1] Dorothy wandered out to the cornfield, where the corn was as high as an elephant's— Well, let's just say the corn was mighty high. Following the rows of corn—and ducking from one row to another—Dorothy arrived at the scarecrow. Toto, her dog, saw a rabbit hopping. With a bark of let-the-hunt-begin, the chase was on.

"Good morning, Scarecrow," brightly greeted Dorothy. "A lovely day for reading." Plopping herself down at the foot of the scarecrow, she leaned against his pole. Often Dorothy would come here to read aloud to him. "Today we're going to read about schools." Taking his silence for consent, she began.

The story she read had a simple idea for schools in Kansas: Let the parents choose. Aunt Em, Uncle Henry, Dorothy and Toto all favored the idea. Money for schooling would be given in the form of an education voucher[2] to parents. Parents could then shop around for a school they liked and send their child there. Simple.

Schools could be private or public. Religious or not. One shade of color or a rainbow of shades. Maybe a school excelling in science, music, or sports. Whatever parents wanted for their children.

"Isn't it wonderful!" said Dorothy, tilting her head up to speak to the scarecrow. The scarecrow nodded his head approvingly in the wind. Leaning back comfortably against the pole, Dorothy closed her eyes to dream about how nice such schools would be. Aunt Em and Uncle Henry would choose a school good for her, not the one that was best for the government.

As Dorothy dozed off, a disquieting spirit came upon her. She saw what today's schools would be like in the future. They were all government-run. Kids were crowded into buses and taken to relocation schools by quotas. Little kids would press their noses against the bus windows and wave good-by to the mother who loved them.

Before entering the huge concrete schools with no windows, each child was searched to see if unapproved textbooks were being smuggled in. If found, the books were seized and thrown into a bonfire. Uppers, downers, and condoms were returned to junior highers.

Entering the classroom, kids would see a camera in the corner of the ceiling monitoring every move they made. Also, classrooms were bugged to hear if children were prayerfully wishing upon a star!

The problem of what to do with little boys and girls who believed they were "specially created" was finally solved. The answer could be seen billowing from chimneys in the settlements of The Third Wreck and Raving Mad.

Lost in a fitful sleep, Dorothy didn't notice the grass and corn stalks rippling from a south wind. Neither did she hear the low wail of the wind from the north. Toto's barking awoke Dorothy with a jerk.

"A CYCLONE!" she gasped. Hurriedly rising to her feet and clutching her book in one arm and Toto in the other, Dorothy started to rush toward home. It was too late! Caught in the center of the cyclone, she was swirled around and around. She screamed! Higher and higher she rose! Farther! Farther! The cornfield faded from sight. Then suddenly, she felt herself softly lowered—into another corn patch! She was bewildered. "Where am I?"

"In Munchkin Land," replied a voice. Turning, Dorothy saw no one—only a scarecrow some feet away. "Munchkin Land?" repeated Dorothy, hoping to trace the voice answering to the speaker.

"Indeed," came the voice. "The eastern part of the land of Oz." Dorothy looked, her eyes widening. "It couldn't be?" she thought. "A scarecrow . . . *talking!*"

"Welcome," greeted the scarecrow.

"Thank you," said Dorothy, rising. "But where exactly is Munchkin Land?"

"Oh, it's not a place. It's a dimension. It covers Munchkin Land, Oz . . . the whole world. Wherever ordinary people let others do their thinking for them."

"Kansas, too?"

"Most definitely."

"But how do you know this? You're only a scarecrow."

"I read. I want to be a lawyer, but because my brain is made of straw, people laugh at me."

"Well, that's not fair!" exclaimed Dorothy. "I know plenty of people with straw for a brain—and it doesn't keep them from being important."

"That's why they stick me up on this pole—so I can't bother them."

"I'll take you down—and you can be my lawyer."

"I would appreciate that."

Dorothy unhooked the scarecrow. "There. What is your name?"

"Scarecrow. It's simple."

"Then Scarecrow it—" Dorothy stopped abruptly, seeing a strange sight. A black school bus being driven furiously was coming through the corn patch! The driver slammed on the brakes; the bus skidded. As the bus came crashing to a stop, the hood flew off the hinges. Hot water gushed from the radiator.

The sides of the bus quaked—then flopped to the ground. And there standing on the driver's seat—was a WITCH!

"TROUBLEMAKER!" screamed the wicked Witch of government schools. "So . . . you don't like going to my public schools, which are government-run." She was approaching closer. Toto covered his eyes with his paws. "Want to choose your own school, do you?" Now her ugly green face and crooked nose were right in front of Dorothy. "I'll tell you when you shall have freedom of choice . . . NEVER!"

Dorothy trembled once, but only once. "*School vouchers*," spoke the Witch, forming each hated word with venom. "Don't you know the trouble you'd be causing? Given many choices, parents would be confused and not choose wisely. Better to let the Chief Wizard from his courthouse choose, my dear." The Witch smiled slyly.

"But," replied Dorothy, not caving in, "people make hard choices every day. When Munchkins shop, I bet they choose from many kinds of toothpaste on the shelf. But if you were in charge of toothpaste, you would put there only your brand. It would be wrapped in yellow and read *Brand X*."

"Hmmm," muttered the Witch. She had hoped to intimidate Dorothy.

"Also," noted Scarecrow, "choosing a school can't be any harder than choosing a husband or a wife. Yet people some-where do this every day."

"Good, Scarecrow," encouraged Dorothy. Then turning to-ward the Witch, Dorothy added, "Would you want the Chief Wizard to pick out the Munchkin you marry?"

"Funny," retorted the Witch, finding no humor in the re-mark. "In our schools, everyone gets the same education: the rich and poor, the smart and slow, an education that is—"

"Crummy."

"Yes. NO!" quickly corrected the Witch. *Her* pupils are trained like parrots to repeat clichés properly. The Witch con-tinued weaving her words. "You know schools will have to dance to the tune the government pipes—if government hands out money for schooling."

"Which is just what we have today," replied Dorothy. "Gov-ernment pays for public schools, and Munchkins go where they're told and *read* what they're told. That's why I have Scare-crow to help bring—"

"Enough, child," snapped the Witch, not able to get Dorothy to dance. "Would you have public schools a dumping ground for slow learners?"

"Where are Munchkins now who aren't too smart?"

"Hmph." The Witch didn't want to say, "Sitting in public schools."

"Besides," added Dorothy, "if public schools can outshine others in teaching the run-of-the-mill kid or the slow learner, what's wrong with that?"

Better try a new tune, thought the Witch. "Money lures thieves." She tried to purr, but it came out a cackle.

"Public schools prove that!"

"Sweetie, I'm talking about the other thieves. The flimflam man, the huckster will come along wanting parents to sign over vouchers to new schools."

"Uncle Henry says the schools we have cough and sputter like tin lizzies. He says"—here Dorothy lowered her voice and tried to speak gruffly like her uncle—" 'When a new model Thunderbird comes along, grab it.' "

"But dearie," said the Witch, poison floating on her breath, "what if the new schools are not all Thunderbirds?"

"Uncle says"—again Dorothy used her low voice—" 'If an Edsel comes along, it'll disappear . . . because nobody wants it.' "

"Hmmm." The Witch hadn't counted on Dorothy being smart. "Schools will waste good money on advertising."

"Word of mouth is free."

The Witch began circling, looking daggers at Dorothy. "Your good schools will try to woo the good students."

"That's the reward for being a good student."

"Pupils will jump from school to school like pogo sticks."

"Vouchers are given to parents, not to kids."

"Think of the confusion, changing from the old way to the new."

"The change from horse 'n' buggy to merry Oldsmobile was even bigger. Would you keep us in horse 'n' buggy schools?"

"Then *choose!* But first . . . hand over your school money to my government school—then go with empty pockets wherever you want."

"Robber! Give the people's money back to the people."

The Witch was taken back. She had hoped to push Dorothy around, but now felt Dorothy's answers were tweaking her crooked nose! Frustrated, the Witch blurted, "Some parents are too lazy to choose *any* school."

"Then the kids will go to the government school on the corner—which is what you want."

Smiling malevolently, the Witch tried to control her anger. "You don't understand what's at stake, my dear. Schools are monopolies ruled by the Wizard and policed by the State. We force children to choose a government school. So your schools teaching good reading, writing, arithmetic and good character would—to put it simply—destroy us."

"No one is out to destroy your schools," maintained Dorothy. "What we want is to replace bad schools with good schools."

"Still," added Scarecrow thoughtfully, "if government schools can't compete, maybe they should step aside."

"QUIET! Or I'll put a match to you!"

"But he's right," defended Dorothy. "Aunt Em says in a good market the best products last because they meet a need in people. So people buy them. What nobody wants is taken off the shelf. Aunt Em says that's the way it should be—and I think so too."

With piercing eyes, the Witch looked at Dorothy. "So, your Aunt Em has taught you to think, has she? When I get you back in the classroom, I'll subtract that from you in a hurry! You know, of course, that religious schools would get vouchers." The Witch thought she'd stir up some prejudice in Dorothy.

"If they can teach Johnny to read," replied Dorothy openly, "they should get a pat on the back!"

"But why should taxpayers have to pay for your reading, 'riting and—if you choose—religion, when I worked hard to make government schools godless?"

"I pay for *their* schools," said Dorothy matter-of-factly. "Uncle Henry works hard and pays a lot of taxes year after year. That money helps pay for a lot of Munchkins to go to school—even though we don't agree with all the stuff they're being taught."

"Nasty girl!" fumed the Witch, stepping up her attack. "Your schools will have substandard teachers."

"But it seems all the bad teachers are in government schools! Test scores prove that."

"Vouchers will be used as a cover-up for segregation. What about that, my pet?"

Dorothy stood firm. "Do you want good schools? Or do you want children herded into stockyards by quotas and branded *black* Angus, *red* Angus, *brown* Jersey, and *black and white* Holstein? Children aren't cattle."

"Smart aleck! You're exactly *why* we can't have children learning outside of government schools!" Then the wicked

Witch launched her big argument. With a sly smile she asked, "And what about separation of church and state, little one?"[3]

"That's the point!" exclaimed Dorothy, growing more confident all the time. "Give parents a voucher and let them choose. Treat secular and religious schools alike, as *schools*—for that's what they are. A school is a school.[4] If a school teaches religion, that's their business—because government has no say about the fourth *R*. Period."

"The separation," said the clear-thinking Scarecrow, "is to get government *out* of religion, which is God's realm. Separation is to keep the State from trespassing on holy ground!"

"Yes!" said Dorothy forcefully. "Just leave us alone, you . . . *wicked Witch!*"

"CURSE YOU, CHILD!" The Witch's green face turned red with rage. "I can't handle the two of you—one a mischievous child, the other, mattress stuffing! I'm having you taken to the Wizard of Schools himself!" Waving her stick of hickory toward the sky, she chanted:

> Monkey smart, monkey dumb,
> Smart or dumb, monkey come!

Suddenly the sound of flapping wings was heard. The sky over the corn patch darkened as a horde of grotesque Winged Monkeys drew near. They came from high places and union halls. They were attacking!

Quickly Dorothy grabbed Toto. The Winged Monkeys snatched Dorothy and Scarecrow in their claws and began flying them to the courthouse of the Wizard of Schools. He, above all, ruled.

What would happen next?!

Notes

1. L. Frank Baum, *The Wizard of Oz*, Grosset & Dunlap, New York, 1900. Illustrations from the land of Oz (except the Witch) are from the original drawings of W. W. Denslow.

2. **SCHOOL CHOICE WITH VOUCHERS**
   Wrong answer for better schools: "Pour in more money"
   Two scholars, John Chubb and Terry Moe, found no relationship between how well pupils did in school and the following slate of false colorings the establishment has been dwelling on for a decade. Chubb says of these ways to spend money and bloat the bureaucracy:

   > School effectiveness has nothing to do with teacher salaries, with per pupil expenditures, with the size of classrooms, with graduation requirements.
   >
   > > —Knight-Ridder News Service, "Liberals come up with conservative answer to school woes," *The San Diego Union*, June 9, 1990, p. A-8.
   > >   John Chubb is senior fellow at The Brookings Institution, a respected and *liberal* think tank.

   Adds Terry Moe:

   > More money, better people, and more programs will leave the schools just as bureaucratic as they are now.
   >
   > > —Terry Moe, "Choice is the key reform; all else is secondary," *The San Diego Union*, April 28, 1991, pp. C-1, 7.
   > >   Terry Moe is a professor of political science at Stanford University.

   Money: Catholic vs. public schools
   The public schools in San Diego County in 1991 spent $4,880 and the Catholics $2,016 per pupil. Yet the Catholics—with the same percentage of minorities—*outscored* the government-run schools. Nationally, Catholic students outperform public school students by as much as one whole grade level!

   > —See Mike Fredenburg, " 'Choice' offers the best hope for success," *The San Diego Union*, May 12, 1991, p. C-7.

JACK GOLD
Courtesy Kentucky Post

The real problem with public schools

Pinpointing the problem, Terry Moe continues:

> Schools are buried in bureaucracy . . . controlled from the top down by school boards, superintendents, central office bureaucracies, state departments of education, state school boards, state legislatures, and other arms of government.

The answer to good schools

"Eliminate top-down control," Moe goes on to say, and free schools to run things:

> The best way is from the bottom up, by liberating the supply of schools and allowing new organizations to emerge on their own in response to what parents and students want. . . . A choice system does that.

Choice for Chubb and Moe means choosing between public *and private* schools.

In returning schools to parents, teachers, and principals, Chubb and Moe would let each school design its own curriculum and hire the teachers it feels are good. As new ideas and schools emerge in the marketplace, the bad ones would be weeded out, the good ones rewarded.

Polling the people

An academic presentation by Chubb and Moe is in their book, *Politics, Markets, and America's Schools*. Their report on polls:

- A nationwide poll "found that 49 percent of the country is 'more likely' and only 27 percent 'less likely' to vote for a presidential candidate who supports giving parents vouchers to pay for their kids' education." (Gallup, January 1988)
- "Support for choice is highest among the poor and racial minorities." The above candidate would be supported by 61 percent of the "partisan poor." (January 1988, Times Mirror poll)
- An overwhelming "71 percent of the public said yes, parents in this community should have the right to

STEVE KELLEY
Courtesy San Diego Union

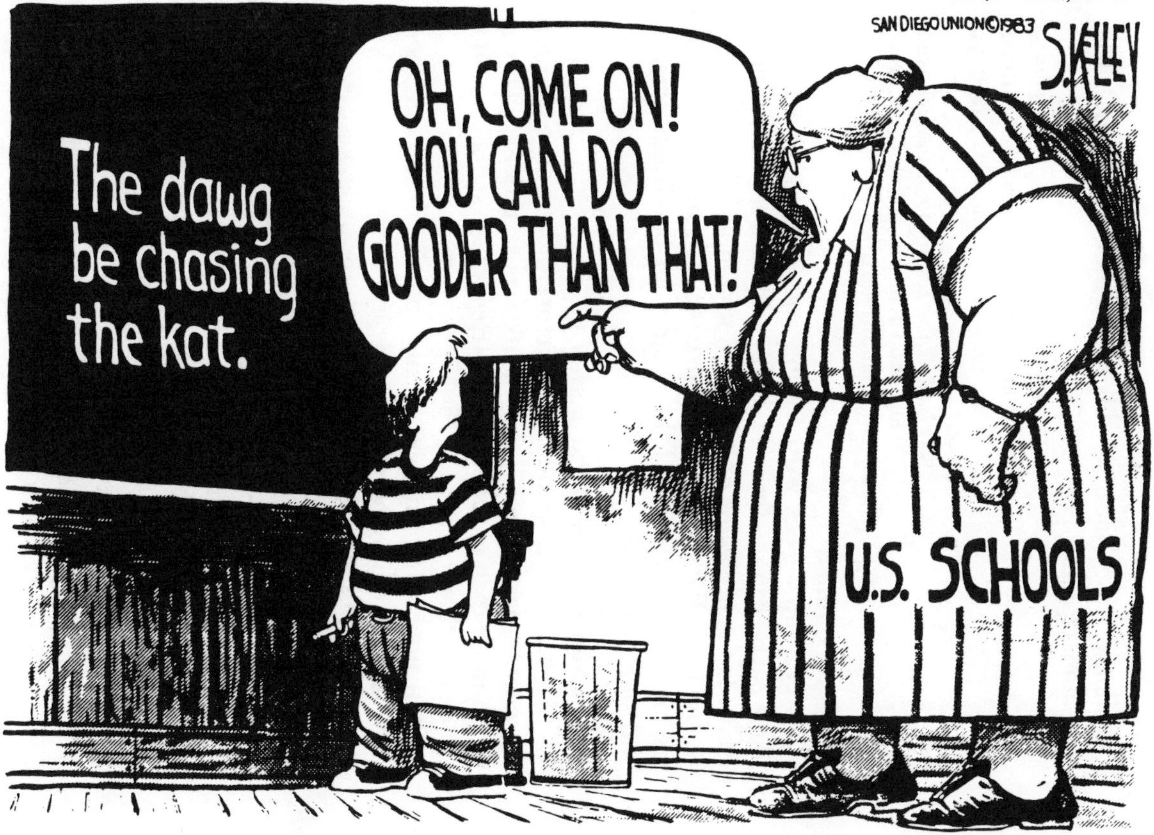

choose which local schools their children attend." (19th Annual Gallup Poll, 1987)

> —John E. Chubb and Terry M. Moe, *Politics, Markets, and America's Schools,* The Brookings Institution, Washington, D.C., 1990, pp. 306–307.
>
> This book is the result of a mammoth study of 500 high schools and 22,000 students, teachers, and administrators.

A second opinion
Chester Finn agrees with Chubb and Moe so often, he is like a partner in the firm of Chubb, Moe & Finn. Chester E. Finn, Jr., is professor of education at Vanderbilt University. In his book *We Must Take Charge* (1991), he fries the following red herrings until they come out pan-fried, black— and smelling fishy.

Fishy: More money is the answer
1) "We have been spending tons more money on education in recent years," says Finn, "$5,638 per student." This is much more than is spent by countries whose schools are doing better than ours. (pp. 76–77)

"I'm not saying 'money doesn't matter,' " he continues. "I'm saying we have no reason to expect more money per se" to make pupils smarter or to know more. (p. 92)

2) Finn quotes a Fordham University professor who finds little money ever reaches the pupil being taught: "Out of the $6107 per student allocated to education by the City of New York, only 32% reaches the classroom." More than half is "lost" to "overhead" before reaching the front school door. Another 17 percent is neatly shifted from teaching to administration. (pp. 76–77)

Fishy: Pay teachers more
"The fact is that teacher earnings have risen a lot in recent years," notes Finn. Teachers make $33,300 for nine months work. Are teachers, then, running to other jobs? No, the turnover rate for public school teachers is quite low:

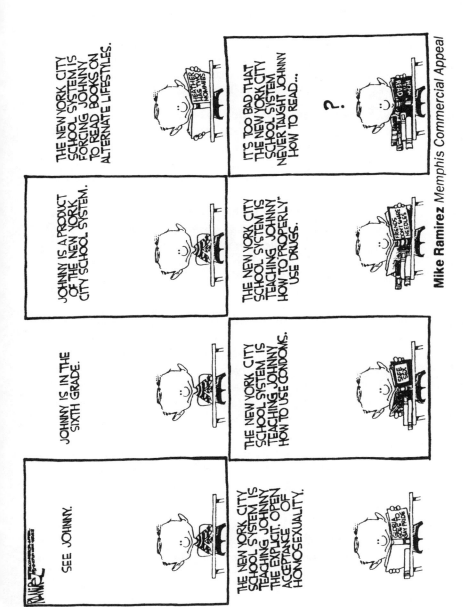

Mike Ramirez *Memphis Commercial Appeal*

The Chicken Littles of the education profession are spreading falsehood when they allege that wretched wages are driving teachers out of education en masse. (pp. 77–79. $33,300 salary on p. 77. $31,278 salary in 1989 on p. 37.)

Fishy: Smaller classes are the answer

If the classes are "below five students"—yes. Smaller classes make teachers and parents happy, Finn believes, and this counts for something. But for academic gain, "reduction of class size is more costly and less effective than other measures . . ." (pp. 80–81)

Sad to say, while classes have been getting smaller and smaller, test scores have been going lower and lower. The number of grade schoolers in a room during 1961 was 30; in 1986, down to 24. In high schools, the teacher's workload per day in 1966 was 130 students; in 1986, down to 105. (pp. 80–81 paraphrased, 293)

The real problem with schools: the education establishment

"Yes, Virginia, there is an 'education establishment.' " So reveals Finn. Further, they are like a horde of Lilliputians tying down schoolboy Gulliver, who has an idea for a new school. Or—if you prefer—they are the special interest groups that block the "Roto-Rooters of reform" from clearing out the stoppages of a school system fit together in the 1800s.

We ought *never* to cede control to the professionals. For the same reason that we do not put doctors in charge of health-care policy . . . soldiers in charge of military policy . . . we are ill-advised to place educators in charge of education policy. . . . Our dreams are not always the subject of their prayers. (p. 243)

Blocking school choice

It is a public policy sin to force a child against her will to attend a dismal school that she and her parents would flee were it not for the coercive power of the state. (p. 262)

Choice in the market place

The market place would work the same for schools as for

restaurants, florists, automobile manufacturers, and magazine publishers. Those institutions that satisfy their customers
flourish and—if they wish—grow. Those that deliver unsatis-
factory products, poor service, or weak value for money must
either change their ways or shrivel and die." (p. 153)

> —Chester E. Finn, Jr., *We Must Take Charge:*
> *Our Schools and Our Future,* The Free Press,
> Macmillan, New York, 1991.

3. **In a letter: A wall of separation to keep government out**

The phrase *wall of separation,* indicating an impassable gulf
between church and state, is nowhere to be found in the
United States Constitution. In fact, the term *church and state*
is lacking in the First Amendment.

The phrases had their origin in a letter written by Thomas
Jefferson. . . . Jefferson rightly places a wall of separation
around the church to protect it from any infringements by the
federal government. That places him in line with the other
founders, who feared the federal government and its possible
attempts to establish a national church.

> —John W. Whitehead, *The Second American*
> *Revolution,* Crossway Books, Westchester, Ill.,
> 1982, pp. 99–100.
>
> John W. Whitehead, founder of the Ruther-
> ford Institute, is a constitutional attorney.

4. **Government: Secular help okay, even if a helping hand for**
religion

In the past, the Supreme Court ruled favorably:
- that a hospital is a hospital—even when run by nuns—so
  building funds were provided by the government. (*Brad-*
  field v. *Roberts,* 1899)
- that public funds may be spent for the safety of children to
  ride public buses to Catholic parochial schools. (*Everson* v.
  Board of Education, 1947)
- that taxes may "benefit the individual" pupil by providing
  secular textbooks to church-related schools. (*Cochran* v.
  Louisiana State Board, 1930)

> —See Robert E. Morgan, *The Supreme Court*
> *and Religion,* The Free Press, New York, 1972,
> pp. 79, 90–93, 100–103.

CHOOSE THE BEST!
SCHOOL VOUCHERS

How can African-American children go to a school where they feel black is beautiful? How can white suburban children get an education based on the Bible? How can atheists go to school and not feel the Hound of Heaven is following, nipping at their heels? How can a feminist parent send her child to a school that understands a feminist view of the world?

Simple. By having a voucher in hand.

What is a voucher?

A voucher is a piece of paper saying the state will pay a child's tuition. The state gathers tax money, then mails out a voucher to the parents of a child in grades kindergarten through 12. The parent gives the voucher to a school, the school mails the voucher to the state, the state sends money to the school.

It is simple and fair if each voucher is made out for the same amount of money and all participating schools, public and private, have the same tuition. One voucher/one tuition. A mother in Watts gets the same voucher as a mother in Beverly Hills.

However, to say, "You can only run your school with voucher money" is self-defeating. All schools, rich and poor, should welcome gifts from alumni, parents and churches, gifts of time, money, and talent, gifts of buildings, endowments, and use of church classrooms.

Some schools may have fees or room and board in addition to tuition. These same schools, however, may offer scholarships. This brings the best schools within reach of the poor.

School printout

A school printout can be modeled after computer printouts for car pools. To receive a printout, a parent could perhaps telephone S-C-H-O-O-L-S.

The printout would include the ten nearest schools for the grade the child is in. If no school is selected from this group, a list of the next ten nearest schools and so forth may be requested.

Private business might bid on handling the printout for a given area. The State would pay the cost. The government's school bureaucracy is not the one to set up the printout.

Schools participating in the voucher program would provide basic information for the printout. Information might include:

- School's philosophy. In one or two sentences, what is the school about—purpose, teaching style, curriculum.
- Location—address, intersection, between what major streets, near what local landmark, in a church or across from a park, etc.
- Public (government-run) or private (privately-run).
- Specialty—science, major sports (football, basketball), art, drama, etc.
- Religious orientation, if any.
- Language(s) spoken in the classroom.
- Number of pupils.
- Number of teachers and their qualifications. A teaching credential is not needed but may be listed as part of a teacher's qualifications.

- Ratio of teachers to pupils.
- Student scores on standard tests.
- Drop-out rate.
- Success rate: students going on to college or vocational skills leading to jobs or what the school feels is success.
- Year school started operating.
- Facilities and dollar value of buildings.
- The school's current costs and income.
- Costs, if any, beyond the tuition.
- Scholarships offered.
- *Optional:* racial and social-economic makeup of the student body.

A general printout will list schools based on geography: the nearest schools. However, parents may pinpoint the type of school they want so the printout is more to their liking.

- OUTLOOK—liberal, conservative, feminist, African-American, etc.
- RELIGION—evangelical, Catholic, Jewish, Black Muslim, atheist, etc.
- SPECIALTY—football, performing arts, science, etc.

Sample: the minischool

"Single-teacher schools, whether held in living rooms, store fronts, or museums, are only one potential type of minischool," report John E. Coons and Stephen D. Sugarman in *Education by Choice*. A minischool may be public or private. They illustrate:

> Mrs. Jones, a ghetto mother, decides to start a school in her apartment for her own four children and half a dozen neighborhood children. Depending on the choice system adopted, Mrs. Jones could qualify, let us say, for from $5,000 to $20,000 in tuition payments from the state. [p. 181. Ten pupils at the 1991 national average of $5,600 spent per pupil would total $56,000.]

Safety standards—drawn up for large public schools—would have to be relaxed for the minischool. But why not?

"After all," continue Coons and Sugarman, "these children already spend most of their time in these same homes with the blessing of the state." (pp. 181–182)

> —John E. Coons and Stephen D. Sugarman, *Education by Choice: The Case for Family Control*, University of California Press, Berkeley, 1978, Part IV, "Designing the Instruments of Choice," pp. 131–211.

Parents may want to do **home schooling** in teaching only their children. If so, there need to be safeguards to keep parents from pocketing the money—or paying off the big-screen TV—and not teaching the children.

First, parents might be required to pass a standard national test covering the level they want to teach—elementary, junior high or high school. A high school diploma may be considered "passing"—certainly at the elementary level—eliminating the test.

Secondly, the children should be given a standard test at the end of each year. The children would have to pass to continue having their parents teach them with voucher money. The voucher payment should be the same, whether a child is taught in a public or private school or in a home.

Private testers could be licensed to give the tests, perhaps as traffic schools are licensed. The parent-teacher would pay a fee for the tests. This would eliminate the bureaucracy of government certifying and molding the parent-teacher into "one of theirs." It also eliminates government snooping into every book used and counting how many days a child attends his home school.

With sensible safeguards, home schooling should be encouraged, particularly in the lower grades. To get started, parents might take a trip to the library and look up "Home Schooling."

"How-to" books list courses for K-12 that follow in sequence what the public school teaches. Christian versions are plentiful. Supplements are discussed: magazines for children, computer software, Bible and music education, and reading lists. Evaluations on which to use are available.

Home teachers might want to begin with a correspondence school for their children until they feel comfortable teaching. They might want to form a "satellite" home school, being related to an established private school. They might want to meet with a home-school support group for encouragement.

Home schooling provides time for lessons in piano, dance, and art. Field trips and trips to the theater are simpler with fewer children.

For social interaction, there are Girl Scouts, Boy Scouts, parks and recreation programs, church groups, girls' softball, Little League baseball, etc. Social interaction does not have to be six hours a day in a blackboard jungle.

> —Much of the home-schooling information is a reflection of *Home Schools: An Alternative* by Cheryl Gorder, Blue Bird Publishing, Tempe, Arizona, 1990.

Returning to Coons and Sugarman, an attractive idea for them is a "personally tailored education" that would bring together independent and perhaps even part-time teachers. They illustrate this minischool:

> Studying reading in the morning at Ms. Kay's house, spending two afternoons a week learning a foreign language in Mr. Buxbaum's electronic laboratory, and going on nature walks and playing tennis the other afternoons under the direction of Mr. Phillips could be a rich package for a ten-year-old. . . . Nor would all children studying with Kay need to spend time with Buxbaum and Phillips; instead some would do math with Mr. Feller or animal care with Mr. Vetter. (p. 182)

At the other extreme is bigness, "the creation of large educational parks." This might appeal particularly to high schoolers. The education park could house public and private schools and single-teacher minischools:

> Each child would be admitted to one school as his home base, but he would have the opportunity to make use of the others

to serve his individual needs. . . . Indeed, such complexes could become beehives of minischools cooperating and competing with one another in the manner of medieval tutors. (pp. 182–183)

Vouchers will give rise to a variety of good schools in a neighborhood, eliminating the need to be bused across town to where chalkboards are imagined to be greener. Neighborhood schools can be reached much as they are now, through school buses, public transportation, cars, car pools, bicycles, and walking. Families can work out as a family or with their chosen school how to reach schools beyond the neighborhood.

Choose the best: the quality schools of today

"Many parents view the public schools as ineffective and dangerous, and are exploring other options before it's too late."

So opens a cover story by *U.S. News & World Report*, December 1991. The news magazine reports that 85 percent of parents in Houston believe their children are unsafe in their public schools. Drugs, violence, bureaucracy, and bad education are creating a flight from public schools. To where?

The article portrays the following as places where baby-boomer parents (paying out of their own pockets) are now sending their children. With voucher money, these quality schools would flourish and be within reach of nearly all children.

1) PREP SCHOOLS. Preparatory schools are nonreligious private schools that prepare a student for college. They emphasize the liberal arts.

Prep schools differ greatly from public schools in teaching. "Dictates don't come down from on high," says Richard Fitzgerald, a headmaster. "There's no school board, no superintendent."

Neither are teachers assigned, based on seniority, from union rolls. Teachers at prep schools are handpicked and given more control over their courses than in government-run schools. Bureaucracy is limited by having teachers handle some administration and having administrators teach.

Teacher salaries average $29,000, compared with nearly $34,000 in public schools. Not as elitist as in the past, prep schools are still expensive, tuition being about $7,000 a year. Scholarships may be available, though, and 100 percent of prep students can plan on going on to college.

2) CHRISTIAN SCHOOLS. Going to a school maintained by a church, a child will have a dress code and expect to study the basics, plus religion or the Bible. Tough classes are encouraged: algebra, advanced English, foreign languages.

Little money is spent on the frills of fancy equipment, elective subjects, and vocational training. Yearly tuition for a Catholic school at the elementary level is about $1,000. At the secondary level about $2,500. (America's 1991 national average spent per pupil: $5,600.)

Little money is spent on bureaucracy. In Washington, D.C., there are 17 central administrators for 50,000 Catholic students compared to 1,500 administrators for 81,000 public school students!

"If a school says, 'Here's what we are, what we stand for,' kids almost always respond to it by working hard," says Paul Hill of the Rand Corporation. He adds, "Catholic schools stand for something; public schools don't."

The results? For graduates of Catholic schools, 83 percent go on to college, compared with only 52 percent for public schools.

3) HOME SCHOOLS. The school day may start in the living room with the Pledge of Allegiance and a prayer. For group activities, the outside resources of a Boys or Girls Club may be used.

"It's easier teaching two kids than it is teaching 35," say two parents who are home teachers. Family values are important to home schoolers, many of whom are conservative Christians, better educated, and more affluent than the national average. Only $400 or $500 a year is spent by a home-schooling family per child.

If teaching continues at the high school level, subjects like calculus, foreign languages and chemistry can be a problem. Still, home-schooled students match or do better than students in the public school on national tests. There is also subjective evidence to think home-schooled pupils are more independent, inquisitive and mature than their public school counterparts.

4) AFRICAN-AMERICAN SCHOOLS. At a private black academy, students wearing green blazers might begin the day standing in front of two flags: a red, black and green African-American flag and a flag of red, white, and blue. Students might then recite "A Pledge to African People."

Seventh graders might be found reading not only Booker T. Washington's *Up From Slavery* but Kipling's *Captains Courageous*. Eighth graders would be learning that tribal blacks also trafficked in slavery.

The aim of most Afrocentric schools is not racial separatism but higher self-esteem and test scores. Learning is so important that Wisconsin State Assembly woman Polly Williams is able to say, "I'm for education, not integration."

Not only have black private schools done well with minority students in the inner-city, but 60 percent of academy students scored above the national averages in reading and math. All this, and the yearly tuition may be as low as $2,000.

5) FOR-PROFIT SCHOOLS. Their budget is met by the tuition fee. "So we put most of our resources into instruction and don't have a lot of frills," says James Williams, headmaster at Gulliver, a for-profit school.

At Gulliver, tuition is about $8,000 a year, and 92 percent of their graduates in 1990 went on to college.

> —The sketch of quality schools is based on the cover story by Thomas Toch, with Betsy Wagner, Constance Johnson, Kukula Glastris in Chicago, Anne Moncreiff Arrarte in Miami,

34

Missy Daniel in Boston and bureau reports, "The Flight from Public Schools," *U.S. News & World Report*, December 9, 1991, pp. 66–77.

A full voucher program can be phased in—high schools and junior highs one year, elementary schools the next, and home schools the following year.

A thought for the school day

The best interests of the child shall be the guiding principle of those responsible for his education and guidance; that responsibility lies in the first place with his parents.

—United Nations Declaration of the Rights of the Child.

Do not conform any longer
to the pattern of this world,
but be transformed
by the renewing of your mind.
—Romans 12:2 NIV

The Scarecrow
and the Wizard of Schools

FLAPPING through the air, the Winged Monkeys approached the courthouse of the Wizard of Schools.[1] In their clutches were Dorothy and Scarecrow. Suddenly, they opened their claws. Dorothy and Scarecrow felt themselves falling! They screamed! Then they realized their fall was soft . . . gentle. They alighted in a planting of marigolds—right outside the courthouse of the Wizard!

Rising to their feet, they went to the Guardian of the Door. "We want to see the Chief Wizard," said Dorothy as bravely as she could. The Guard looked at them a moment. "He's expecting you. Follow me."

Entering the mahogany and marble courtroom, Dorothy saw the Chief Wizard behind his bench. He was much taller than Munchkins, which is perhaps why he ruled. Alongside him were his eight little benchmarks, four on each side.

Munchkins packed the courtroom as spectators, some were sitting on red-cushioned pews, others standing. Munchkins look like ordinary people, only smaller and with a pink complexion. They were hoping for . . . anything better.

Dorothy stared at the Chief Wizard. He wore a common black robe. He was bald on top with white hair along the sides of his head. He looked . . . so ordinary.

"*He* picks my school," thought Dorothy, disappointed. He didn't look any different than her granddaddy the day he was taken off to the convalescent home.

"I am the Great and Terrible Wizard," intoned the Chief of the court. "What is it you want?"

"I want to choose my own school," said Dorothy flatly.

"You live in Kansas?"

"Yes, and I'm tired of being bused across town away from Aunt Em, Uncle Henry, and all my friends."

"Quiet, child! Children of all the same color go to schools near you."

"But they're good schools!"

"Schools are good if they teach what the State wants taught. I repeat my earlier ruling." The Wizard rose to his feet. "Separate but equal is inherently unequal in education!"[2]

"Ridiculous," muttered Dorothy.

The Wizard was stunned. Nobody in years had questioned his ruling, much less a child. "What did you say?" he asked, more curious than indignant.

"I said *Ridiculous*. My teacher and I had lunch together one day. She split a Hershey bar in half, sharing six squares with me and keeping six squares for herself. Now you stand there and tell me the chocolate bar my teacher cut into separate but equal pieces is unequal? Hogwash! Who was discriminated against— me or my teacher?"

The Wizard shifted uneasily, smiling weakly at his associates. "She's . . . only a child," he assured his little benchmarks.

"Also, Don and Jimmy brought a sack of 12 marbles to school one day. Taking turns choosing, they each chose the six marbles they wanted. The dozen marbles were divided fair and square—separately and equally. Now you stand there and say *No*. So tell me, who got cheated, Don or Jimmy?"

An uneasiness arose in the courtroom. Some Munchkins began to wonder, "Is truth in the field of math not truth in the field of education?" Others wondered, "Is this any way to run a country, where $1 + 1 = 2$ outside the schoolroom but not in the schoolroom?"

"My ruling is made," replied the Wizard, smoothing things over and not wanting the Munchkins to hear a different opinion. "To carry out my plan in Oz, we put children who are light pink in color on yellow buses[3] and drive them to little red schoolhouses filled with children who are deep pink. Then we turn these yellow buses around and drive the deep pink children to little red schoolhouses filled with children who are light pink. Surely you can understand that?"

"You've turned schools into bus stops!" exclaimed Dorothy. "And why? Being smart has no color. Why can't a teacher who is deep pink teach as well as a teacher who is light pink? And why are deep pink kids always made to feel dumb? A kid is a kid. There are light pink kids who are smart, and some who are dumb. There are deep pink kids who are smart, and some who are dumb."

"Heh-heh-heh," nervously laughed the Chief Wizard. Looking again at his eight little benchmarks, he tugged at his collar, which was becoming increasingly hot. "Just a child," he reminded his associates.

"Nevertheless," he uncomfortably continued, "what's done is done. To make sure everyone has the same secular education in humanism, I have introduced a new racial program. Every Munchkin is now stamped as one of the following:

> Light pink
> Pretty pink
> Not-so-pink
> Deep pink.

"The State must be careful about who's who in the classroom. That is why . . . a sweet girl like you . . . goes to the school you do." The Wizard grimaced in pain, thinking he was smiling.

"Samuel was a judge. He said people look at the outside of a person, but God looks on the heart."[4]

"Samuel . . . yes. But he never made it to the Supreme Court!" joked the Wizard. His benchmarks smiled, but the Munchkins in their seats were too disenchanted to smile. They knew thinking like Dorothy's had been erased from their minds like so much chalk from a chalkboard.

"If I may speak on Dorothy's behalf," said the Scarecrow.

"Who are you?" asked the Wizard, growing tired of being put on the spot.

"I'm Scarecrow, Dorothy's lawyer. I wish to mention that our Charter does not mention the words *education* or *school*."

"So?"

"So anything not mentioned as belonging to the government belongs to the people. This is written in the 10th Right."[5]

"So what?"

"So Aunt Em, Uncle Henry, and Munchkins everywhere can run their own schools—without government meddling."

"Hmph. Read that Charter all you want, but you don't know what the words mean until I tell you what they mean!"[6] The Wizard was starting to get angry.

"And on the matter of wishing upon a star," continued Scarecrow, undaunted. "Our 1st Right says that *no law* shall be passed—"[7]

"I remind everyone in this courtroom," loudly called out the Wizard, "that I interpret *no law* to mean *any law* I feel is best for you may be passed."[8]

Scarecrow continued his carefully charted course. "About only Congress being able to make laws—"[9]

"If a law doesn't suit me,' interrupted the Wizard, "I'll throw it out!"

"About the book, *Who Made the Munchkins?*—"

"Stop bothering me about that book! I repeat: The Maker's book may be used in school for its history and literary merit, but not for devotion.[10] I guess that makes it clear who rules its pages. Me. I tell you, I'm the Chief Wizard and THERE IS NONE HIGHER IN THE LAND!" Eight little pairs of hands went clap-clap-clap as the eight little benchmarks applauded their wonderful wiz.

"Phooey!" said Dorothy simply, expressing what Munchkins there were thinking.

"You, sir," quietly resumed Scarecrow, "stand where you are by the grace of these good people." Scarecrow indicated the Munchkins present, who looked at each other in great surprise.

"Is it not true that an **amendment to the Charter**[11] can be passed, returning schools to the people? And is it not true that the founding fathers wanted schools run at the grassroots, which is where their school bells rang?"[12]

The Wizard shifted uneasily. "It is," he admitted, not quite knowing what was coming.

"Cannot an amendment be passed by these very Munchkins?" Scarecrow took from his pocket a folded piece of paper and read his proposed amendment:

> Parents are to be given an Education Voucher for the
> public or private schooling of their child in grades kin-
> dergarten through twelve. Schools are solely in charge of
> their teaching philosophy, religious orientation if any,
> textbooks, teachers hired, and students accepted. The
> Voucher, given by the state, is to equal the cost of one
> year's education in the public schools of that state.

"They may," replied the Wizard, playing it casually and being seated. "But with me guiding—"

"Munchkins," said Scarecrow, addressing those present, "public and private schools have already been tested, for both have been around for many years. After the amendment is passed, provinces in Oz may simply be given a number of years to implement the *people's choice.*"

"Good, Scarecrow," encouraged Dorothy.

The Wizard thought he'd better take charge once more. Starting to rise, he said, "Now see here—"

"And is it not true," challenged Scarecrow, "that lawmakers can **curb what this court can rule on?** Is it not true that the court is not a church—that you cannot say how the book *Who Made the Munchkins?* can be read, or when and where children may wish upon a star?"

Growing a little pale, the Chief Wizard returned to sitting.

"And is it not true that *no law* means *hands off!*[13] Cannot lawmakers pass the following into law?" Looking at the paper from his pocket, Scarecrow read:

> Courts are forbidden to meddle in or rule on worship,
> prayer, sacred writings, and the teaching of religion.

"See here—"

"*Is it not true?!*"

"Of course it is," confessed the Wizard, again sinking into his chair. He looked at his eight little benchmarks, who were sliding down on their chairs, hoping not to be seen. *When I need them*, thought the Wizard, *how silent they are.*

"Cannot lawmakers **pass a new law or amend an old one?**"

"If they want," shrugged the Wizard, dismissing the matter lightly.

"Cannot **justices be impeached?**" Turning to the Munchkins, Scarecrow explained, "Grounds for impeachment are 'treason, bribery, or other high crimes and misdemeanors.'[14] On a scale of *one* to *ten*, treason is a *ten*, misdemeanors a *one*. On the same scale, the Maker's book—"

"I've had enough of this!" said the Wizard rising and realizing things had gotten serious. "Deputies, arrest this man!"

The deputies looked at each other, then walked over to the Munchkins to take their stand with the people. Flabbergasted, the Wizard looked to his eight little—now seven little—benchmarks. One had quietly slipped away. Two other benchmarks came over and whispered encouragement to the Wizard to carry on. Pretending dignity, they then walked out.

"Is it not true," challenged Scarecrow forcefully, "that having **confirmed justices once,** a law can be passed to have them **reconfirmed** seven years later, when it is found out what wisdom they really have? And would this not spare us the shaky rulings of a Chief Justice Alzheimer?"

"It . . . might," replied the Wizard, not fully listening. He was worriedly watching as another benchmark deserted him.

"Tell us more," shouted a Munchkin, breaking their silence in the courtroom.

"Yes! More!" agreed other Munchkins.

"You may **require more than one vote** for the court to decide," Scarecrow informed them. "One *opinion* (5–4) can tear up what your lawmakers have written."

With great fervor, Scarecrow began to conclude. "Munchkins, do you want to thumb through the newspapers each Monday to see what the latest truth is? Separate is equal one day, unequal the next. Wouldn't you rather have a nation run by law than ruled by the Opinion of the Day? The Charter is stable;

Wizards fly in the wind. Lawmakers are elected; Wizards have to be carried out feet first.

"Munchkins, *you* are the rulers—only you don't know it! Take back your schools! Take back your book *Who Made the Munchkins?* Take back wishing on a star! THEY BELONG TO YOU!"

Wagging his tail excitedly, Toto grabbed the hem of the Wizard's robe in his teeth. "Grrrr." Toto was trying to pull the Wizard out of the courtroom!

"Hooray for Scarecrow!" shouted one bearded Munchkin.

"Let's make him our new Chief!"

"Our new Chief!" echoed all the Munchkins.

"No!" cried the Wizard. He shot up so abruptly, his robe being pulled by Toto slipped to the floor.

"Look!" cried out a Munchkin.

There for everyone to see was a Munchkin—no bigger than any of them—but standing on a ladder! He felt small indeed. Looking around, he saw all his benchmarks had fled. He was alone.

"Why, you're a HUMBUG!" said Dorothy flatly.

"I am," he replied, hanging his head. "I'm a common man. An ordinary Munchkin." Knowing his flimflam was over, he climbed down.

"No one higher . . . hmph!" groused an old Munchkin, expressing what other spectators were thinking and feeling.

The grounded Wizard—standing before Dorothy and having to look up—offered apologetically, "Perhaps I overreached a little. . ."

"A LITTLE?! Shame on you! You're a very bad man."

"No," softly replied the Wizard. "I like to think of myself as a good man—just a bad Wizard."

"Well, now the people have Scarecrow—a good and wise man who will answer to Munchkins."

"A good man he is," agreed the Munchkins, flocking around Scarecrow and congratulating him for scaring away the crows of tyranny and fear that pecked away their harvest.

"It's about time," said one Munchkin woman with finality.

"It's about time . . .

"It's about time . . .

"It's about time I found you. Land sakes, child, let a person know where you're going."

Dorothy blinked her eyes. It was Aunt Em! Looking up, Dorothy saw the scarecrow against which she had fallen asleep. Could it have been . . . a dream! Picking up her book, Dorothy rose to her feet.

"And don't forget this paper you stuck in the scarecrow's pocket." Aunt Em lifted the folded paper from the scarecrow's old coat and handed it to Dorothy.

"I didn't write any paper," remembered Dorothy. Unfolding the paper, she saw it was not even in her handwriting! The paper began:

> Parents are to be given an Education Voucher for the public or private schooling of their child . . .

Dorothy's mouth fell open as she stared at the scarecrow. Gathering her senses, Dorothy said softly, "Thank you, Scarecrow. From all of us Munchkins."

Notes

1. L. Frank Baum, *The Wizard of Oz*, Grosset & Dunlap, New York, 1900. Illustrations are from the original drawings of W. W. Denslow. The Scarecrow with a sheet of paper is a composite.

2. **Separate but equal**

   "We conclude that in the field of public education the doctrine of 'separate but equal' has no place. Separate educational facilities are inherently unequal."

   > —Chief Justice Earl Warren in Robert Shnayerson, *The Illustrated History of the Supreme Court of the United States,* Harry N. Abrams, Inc., New York, 1986, p. 226.

   Separate but superior
   In a 1987 experiment, Florida opened two all-black, all-male classrooms in kindergarten and first grade. The boys, who had no father in the home, were given a black teacher as a role model.

   Up went attendance. Up went test scores. Down came the Government-as-Schoolmaster, explaining in effect: Schools are for integration, not learning. Go back to your government-integrated schools where attendance is low, scores are low, and from where one out of four black men can expect in age 20–29 to be in jail, on probation, or on parole.

   > —"Fighting the Failure Syndrome," *Time,* May 21, 1990, pp. 83–84.

3. A unanimous Burger Court ruled busing and racial quotas could be used to desegregate schools in *Swann* v. *Charlotte-Mecklenburg (N.C.) County Board of Education* (1971).

   > —In *The Supreme Court: Justice and the Law,* third edition, Congressional Quarterly Inc., Washington, 1983, p. 60.

   Busing: going nowhere
   A model of integration, of busing, is Charlotte, N.C. But after 17 years, what do the parents think?

> *Whites:* "Our kids aren't getting the same education [as in other schools]. That creates particular resentment among the whites who are left in the system to keep it integrated."
> *Blacks:* "At the end of the bus ride, where are we at?"

At the end of ever earlier and longer busing, disillusioned blacks arrive at high schools where academic classes end up mainly white and where slow learners in skill classes are mainly black.

> —"Busing: How to Get Everyone Mad," *Newsweek,* March 7, 1988, pp. 39, 40.

On the West Coast, the story is the same. San Diego schools have spent *$500 million* on integration over the last two decades—mostly on busing. The results?

- Minorities bused to white schools score lower than minorities who stay in inner-city schools.
- "We've been at this for 25 years and what have we achieved? I don't honestly know."
   > —Irma Castro, former president of the local Chicano Federation.
- "The kids go to what looks like an integrated school, but when the bell rings they go into different classrooms."
   > —Elaina Hershowitz, an administrator in the county Office of Education.
- At a posh white school in La Jolla, whites fear that integrated classes will be "watered-down." So an English class that is half Latino is watching a video of "The Legend of Sleepy Hollow." Next door is an English class with no Latinos. They are reading 17th century poetry.
- At lunch in the above school, Latinos eat together in a corner of the courtyard. They call the other side of the courtyard where whites gather, "Whiteland."
- "They [bused minorities] have never achieved in the receiving schools, and we have the test scores to prove it."
   > —Pat Meredith, vice principal of Lewis Junior High School and president of the Association of African-American Educators.

BOB MURPHY
Courtesy Manchester Union-Leader

- In San Francisco, schools must juggle *three or four* ethnic groups, with no one group being more than 45 percent. In La Crosse, Wisconsin, a mandatory busing program was begun to integrate *rich* kids with *poor* kids!

> —Above information on San Diego comes from a three-part series. Maura Reynolds, "Integration's failures shake schools' faith," *The San Diego Union-Tribune,* December 2, 1992, pp. A-1, 14. December 3, 1992, pp. A-1, 13. December 4, 1992, pp. A-1, 6.

Busing rolls on—Music crashes

Fueled by millions of dollars, busing burns up money that could go elsewhere.

The scene was the Harlem School of the Arts in New York City. A teenager came to audition for the Concert Chorale, a chorus of 35 singers. His moment came. He began to rap, not sing.

"He didn't know the difference between singing and talking," said Betty Allen, president and former executive director of the school. "That's a direct result of the fact that in 1977 New York City eliminated music teachers from elementary schools and all but a few in the upper schools and specialized schools."

> —William H. Honan, "Performing arts shifting from serious to stylish," New York Times News Service, *The San Diego Union-Tribune,* January 5, 1993, p. E-5.

Busing: Black parents are coming home

It's in a tough neighborhood of Chicago. Yet at Dumas Elementary School with an enrollment of 682, you will find no graffiti on the walls nor violence in the halls.

What you will find are kids listening to Mozart in their music class and tackling Latin in fifth grade. Danielle, 6, is able to recite two poems by Langston Hughes. You will also hear the kids being told, "You've got to move your buns!"

Dumas is all black. A public school, Dumas is still testing below the state average. But their attendance is a whopping 94 percent, they have a waiting list, and they have 60 parents volunteering on a given day.

"Black parents who bused their kids are coming home," says black principal Sylvia Peters. "Forget the idea that black children can't learn unless they're sitting next to a white child. Some values are universal, like self-love, respect, integrity and perseverance."

> —"The Bus Doesn't Stop Here," *Time*, December 17, 1990, p. 102.

Reading, 'riting, 'rithmetic—or riding?

Scholar John Chubb feels the busing issue needs to be faced squarely:

> What are we interested in, good schools or simply racially mixed schools, because they may be at odds with one another.

Yet Chubb—who believes choice in the market place will create quality schools—feels learning and desegregation can walk hand in hand:

> If you have lots of quality schools—and that's the idea here, to create lots of quality schools—I think people of different races are more likely to be willing to go to school together than if you've got lots of crummy schools and you're trying to compel people to go.

> —In an interview with the Knight-Ridder News Service, "Liberals come up with conservative answer to school woes," *The San Diego Union*, June 9, 1990, p. A-8.
>
> John Chubb is a senior fellow at The Brookings Institution.

4. I Samuel 16:7.
5. Amendment Ten of the Constitution:

> The powers not delegated to the United States by the Constitution, nor prohibited by it to the States, are reserved to the States, respectively, or to the people.

It reads: "to the people" not "to the Court." The Constitution with the Bill of Rights begins "We the people" and ends "to the people."

6. Who rules America—judges or the people?

Judges

"The Constitution is what the judges say it is."

> —Chief Justice Charles Evans Hughes in John W. Whitehead, *The Stealing of America*, Crossway Books, Westchester, Ill., 1983, p. 25.
> John W. Whitehead, founder of the Rutherford Institute, is a constitutional attorney.

Not the Judges

"Any broad unlimited power to hold laws unconstitutional . . . was not given by the Framers, but rather has been bestowed on the Court by the Court."

> —Justice Hugo Black in John W. Whitehead, *The Second American Revolution*, Crossway Books, Westchester, Ill., 1982, pp. 70–71.

"[For] 150 years the Court was content with the policing function . . . It fell to the Warren Court to take the lead in deciding what national policy ought to be when the legislative and executive failed to act. But the failure of Congress to exercise legislative power does not vest it in the Court."

> —Harvard professor Raoul Berger in *Second*, p.52.

The People

"The Constitution ought to be preferred to the statute, the intention of the people to the intention of their agents.

"Nor does this conclusion by any means suppose a superiority of the judicial to the legislative power. It only supposes that the power of the people is superior to both. . ."

> —Alexander Hamilton, *The Federalist Papers*, in *Supreme Court* (Congressional Quarterly), p. 45.

"This government of the people, by the people, for the people."

> —Abraham Lincoln, "Gettysburg Address."

"Return government to the people. They have a right to govern themselves and to make their own mistakes."

> —Harvard professor Raoul Berger in *Second*, p. 72.

7. Amendment One of the Constitution:
> Congress shall make no law respecting an establishment of religion, or prohibiting the free exercise thereof . . .

8. **Landmark: Government forbids free exercise of prayer**
Defying the 1st Amendment, government-as-god thundered a new commandment from Mt. Washington. With a judges-know-best mentality, they ruled in essence, "No prayer between 9:00 a.m. and 3:00 p.m. No prayer on school grounds."

With their new commandment, the new gods *established* that voluntary prayer in *the free exercise of religion* should be *prohibited!* They feebly reasoned that prayer brings:
> indirect coercive pressure upon religious minorities to conform to the prevailing officially approved religion . . .
> > —*Engel* v. *Vitale*, 1962, in Shnayerson, p. 240.

A balanced judgment
If the Court could establish religion—and it cannot—it should have used "balance" and concluded:
> The religious freedom of tens of millions of Americans who want prayer and Bible reading in schools of choice outweighs the religious freedom of one atheist, two Unitarians, and ten others in government schools who don't.
> > —See "balance" in *American Communications Association* v. *Douds*, 1950, and *Barenblatt* v. *United States*, 1959, in Shnayerson, pp. 215 and 227.

Reindeer ruling
Young gods abound, like the judges in Rhode Island who made the "reindeer ruling." With the brilliance of Santa Claus, they favored a secularized nativity scene.

For instance, what would be allowed is a town-supported nativity scene—if you don't mind the manger being Santa's cottage. Or Joseph standing while holding a shepherd's staff . . . that is a candy-striped cane. Or the Holy Family surrounded by woolly sheep . . . the wool being yummy cotton candy. Or the Holy Family awaiting the coming of

WAYNE STAYSKAL
Courtesy Tampa Tribune

three, racially-balanced kings (white, black, and yellow) who come riding in on—are you ready for this?—three reindeer. Get the idea?

—See *Time*, December 12, 1988, p. 71.

Nativity scenes and menorahs

Like prayer and the Bible, nativity scenes and Hanukkah menorahs are religious. The Court may not rule on them. Crèches and candelabrums may be displayed on private property. Persons wanting to display these religious symbols on public property—such as in parks and civic centers—enter the things that are Caesar's and need to ask the local governing authorities for a permit.

The civil authorities (not the courts) may say yes or no, depending on local customs and what advantages or disadvantages they feel the displays have for their community. A Jewish community may say "No" to a nativity and "Yes" to a menorah. An atheistic community may say "No" to both. This is proper.

If a majority of people are unhappy with the decision, they may elect new (local) rulers who will reflect the will of the people. "Majority rules" in a democracy, and good leaders rule all the people with wisdom and compassion.

A nation ruled by Santas

The Supreme Court does not have to be made up of lawyers, who are trained in law. Such a court is ignorant of schooling and religion, nongovernment matters that belong to the people. Little wonder these phony Santas have turned schools and prayer into Halloween.

9. Article I section 8 (18) of the U.S. Constitution.
10. School District of *Abington Township* v. *Schemp* (1963) in Shnayerson, p. 240.
11. See *Supreme Court* (congressional Quarterly), pp. 53–69.
12. **How American schools began**

America began its remarkable history without public education—with the exception of some local common schools in

New England. The federal Constitution does not even mention education, and it certainly does not enumerate a federal power to aid or regulate education. From the beginning of this country, education was an area of concern left to the families and churches in the individual states. At that time, education was almost exclusively private, although it was often financially aided by the state.

—John W. Whitehead, *Stealing*, p. 83.

13. **The Supreme Court, Congress, and the President may not rule *yes* or *no* on religion**

"[The purpose of the First Amendment was] to exclude from the national government all power to act on the subject . . . of religion."

—Edward S. Corwin, constitutional law authority. In *Second*, p. 100.

"There is not a shadow of right in the general [federal] government to intermeddle with religion. . . . This subject is, for the honor of America, perfectly free and unshackled. The government has no jurisdiction over it."

—James Madison in *Second*, p. 100.

14. **The United States Constitution. Article II section 4.**

Thou hast created all things,
and for thy pleasure
they are and were created.
—Revelation 4:11 KJV

The Spirit of the Arts

WHAT IS ART?

Open, ye heavens, your living doors; let in
The great Creator from his work returned
Magnificent, his six days' work, a world.
—John Milton[1]

ART[2] is the outward expression of an inner vision.[3] Like a
spark, it springs from the imagination of the artist and touches
the soul of the beholder.

Art may be primitive—a toddler splashing red and yellow
paint on a sheet of white paper, then proudly holding up the
mouse-terpiece and entitling it "mommy and daddy." This is
a toddler who may one day grow up to be another Grandma
Moses.

A work of art can be artistically authentic or vital without being
great or profound. . . . But to be *real* art, whether it be profound or slight, it must be freshly and honestly conceived and
executed. The crude art of children often has this quality, as

does the art of many adult artists whose craftsmanship and whose insights are more or less inadequate.[4] (Paul Tillich)

Art may also be sophisticated, like the "Toccata and Fugue in D Minor" by organ-*Meister* Bach.

Art brings a dance to our toes, a poem to our hearts, a melody to our lips, a painting to our eyes, and a drama to our minds. Artist and beholder are swept up as one. And there is evening and there is morning . . . we are awakened.

CREATOR OF THE ARTS

Be glad and rejoice forever
in what I am creating.
—Isaiah 65:18 New RSV

The creator of the arts is God. He is the first Artist, the supreme Sculptor. Long before God created Adam, he created angels and the arts.

Then the seven angels who had the seven trumpets prepared to sound them.[5]

Then I looked and heard the voice of many angels, numbering thousands upon thousands. . . . In a loud voice they sang . . . [6]

The ancient structures of art were placed into the foundation of our world during the six days of creation.[7] Like the structures of government and education, they were placed here as part of earth's fullness. As God fashioned the arts, he left his imprint on his creation. He created people in his image to speak, to sing, to dance . . . to reason and act out performances. As producer, God picked Adam to be the first playwright and casting director on earth.

[God brought animals] to Adam to see what he would call them; and whatever Adam called every living creature, that was its name.[8]

As God worked, he quickened and awakened the colossal frameworks he earlier had created, adapting them to fit his new creation of clay. Humans may not have the voice range of angels, but we would make a joyful noise. Humans may not fly through the air,[9] but we would dance. When did dance begin on earth? Writes van der Leeuw, a Dutch theologian:

> God moved, and he set us upon this earth in motion. . . . It is the beginning of his work in creation and salvation. It is also the beginning of the dance.[10]

Drama? Drama began with God seeking man, and man either rebelling or returning. Man rebelling is tragedy. Man returning is divine comedy. Design?

> The blueprint must have proceeded unconsciously from that well-built city whose artist and architect is God.[11]

Music?

> The echo of the eternal Gloria.[12]

God created the arts, so he is king over all the arts and savior of fallen arts.[13]

Art arises from one of three spirits—the spirit of God, the human spirit, or the spirit of Satan. It is common for the human spirit to mingle with either of the other two spirits. This blended art may be said to be "prompted" or "inspired" by God or Satan. Art may start off with the human spirit but then be joined to a high or low degree by God and/or Satan. The art work then ends up with mixed spirits.

The following are not neat little boxes, but are guidelines for discerning what spirit (or spirits) is present in art.

GODLY ART
Soli Deo Gloria[14]

Art is godly if it is God's handiwork—his many-splendored creations—or if it shares in his beauty. It is what the hand of God forms directly, or indirectly through the hand of his artist.

God chooses an artist,[15] fashions and purifies him into an instrument fit for his use, then anoints him. God may use the artist for a time, the artist choosing to go his own way before or afterwards. Saul of Tarsus, a persecutor early in life, was later to write marvelous letters under the pen name Paul. The Italian opera composer Puccini late in life wrote to a friend:

> Almighty God touched me with his little finger and said "Write for the theater—mind, only for the theater." And I have obeyed the supreme command.[16]

God may work through a corner of the artist's soul during the day, while the artist swaggers through a Red Light district at night. But leading a double life, as gospel singer and preacher Jimmy Swaggart discovered, is a life with its days numbered.

Clay is imperfect; it tends to sag, crumble or crack. But clay is what God uses. Being chosen and used of God does not mean an artist is perfect, cleansed for more than a moment, or used for life. The psalmist David, for instance, was an adulterer and a murderer.[17] Still, he was a poet par excellence for God, for he was chosen and willing to write great thoughts about God.

Being an artist for the Author of life means the artist is rooted in his Maker. God is the vine; we are the branches.[18] There is harmony and wholeness—oneness. Like fruit forming on the vine, art flows through the hands of the artist. Works of the godly artist are marked by

Love
Joy[19]
Peace
Patience
Kindness
Goodness

Faithfulness
Gentleness
Self-control[20]
. . . all reflected in splendid forms.

"God gave me this poem," says a beginning poet, "and I wrote it in only three minutes!" The best reply seems to be, "God gave it to you, not to the world." A gift to an individual may not be a calling to the world of arts. A wide-eyed beginner receives a flash of inspiration and feels what is entrusted to him or her is Holy Scripture, with not a word to be added or taken away.[21] A master writer looks at what the newborn poet wrote and whimsically recognizes it to be refrigerator art—childlike art posted on the door of a refrigerator.

Generally, God gives beginners rough drafts, not final forms. In a calling, the artist is led by the Holy Spirit as talent, knowledge, discipline, craft, critiques, and rewrites come into play. The cost of discipleship needs to be paid.[22]

God has a viewpoint on all subjects, religious and secular. He created the secular world; it belongs to him. The opposite of *sacred* is not *secular* but *profane*. Subjects like sex and money are fit subjects for the godly artist.[23]

Created good but fallen, the secular world needs to be restored, not ignored. Certainly it is a world that should not be handed over to Satan as a plaything.

Religious subjects may not be godly art. Sunday school pictures, butterflies and sweetness may or may not be godly art. Shallow form or spirit is not even good art. The godly artist works from the depth of his being and soars past earth to the realm where God dwells.

[In Mozart's "Champagne Song" from *Don Giovanni*,] there is more depth, more awareness of the holy, than in many an oratorio or hymn. When we come to fundamentals, the "last word" about champagne is nearer to the word of God than is an empty word about God. . . .

"Religious" music in the true, deep sense is not only the music of Bach and Palestrina, but also a symphony of Beethoven, an opera of Mozart, a waltz of Strauss. All music that is absolute music, without additions, without anything counterfeit, is the servant of God; just as pure painting is, whether it treats religious subjects or not; and as true architecture is, apart from the churches it builds . . . [24] (van der Leeuw)

It does not follow from this that there is no such thing as Christian art. Some modern Christians—in the popular fashion of the day—look at the designation *Christian art* and scoff, "Too narrow. Too intolerant." Art is Christian if it reflects a New Testament world-view and bears the fruit of the Holy Spirit.

Christ has been pushed out of creation in the minds of many people. While the Father is the master designer and the Holy Spirit the quickening spirit, it is the Christ who was and is the instrument of creation, the shaping hand.

All things were made by him; and without him was not any thing made that was made. [25]

"My Father has worked [even] until now.—He has never ceased working, He is still working—and I too must be at [divine] work." [26]

In a perfect book, we might think of the Father as the timeless idea for the book, the Son as the writing of the book as well as the Word on the page, and the indwelling Spirit as the reading of the book, bringing it to life, bringing a response from the reader. [27]

In a symphony written by a godly spirit, we might identify the Father with the complete idea, at once containing the beginning and the end of the work. The Son might be regarded as the composer who takes airy notes, makes them incarnate on paper, and then chooses, trains and conducts the orchestra. The

Holy Spirit might be thought of as quickening the music in the hearts and minds of players of strings, horns, and percussion, as well as in making the music come alive in listeners, who then respond to the Makers of music.

There is something wrong with theories of art that have "no room" for the Son, the Christ of history.[28]

HUMAN ART

Know then thyself, presume not God to scan;
The proper study of mankind is man.
Placed on this isthmus of a middle state,
A being darkly wise and rudely great:

. . .

He hangs between; in doubt to act or rest;
In doubt to deem himself a god, or beast;

. . .

Created half to rise, and half to fall;
Great lord of all things, yet a prey to all;
Sole judge of truth, in endless error hurled;
The glory, jest, and riddle of the world!
—Alexander Pope[29]

Human art bears the fruit of the human spirit. The human spirit is concerned with the earth, with treasures in the earthly form of

Peace
Freedom
Power
Love
Belonging (friends, family, country)
Wealth
Culture
Health
Sex.

These are treasures as the world gives them—and takes them away. Just as a husk is needed to house a kernel of grain until it becomes golden, so earthly things house and enrich the human spirit and soul.[30]

All those born of earth belong to the brotherhood of man. Human art, as such, is not concerned with the second, spiritual birth, which places people into the family of God under the fatherhood of God. It pays no mind to the spirit realm, a world of angels and demons, a land of heaven and hell. It fancies a world of *you* and *me* in a land of clay.

Yet the proper way to serve the world is to seek first the kingdom of God, be filled with the Creator's spirit, and then go—paintbrush in hand—into the world to serve. A person going it alone has fewer brushes, fewer colors, and a smaller vision.

The arts—created good but fallen—are, in a sense, neutral.[31] They are the stuff of life available for use. Human art may range from awful to beautiful, depending on the talent and spirit of the artist and whether the spirit of God or Satan is mingled with the work.

Richard Wagner was a composer. He was also ruthless, amoral, arrogant, and a racist—something of a messianic lunatic.

> "I will destroy the existing order of things."
> "I am the German spirit. Consider the incomparable magic of my works."
> "I am being used as the instrument of something higher than my own being warrants."[32]

Adolph Hitler liked that kind of thinking. He used Wagner's music to trumpet the Third Reich.

It also happens that Wagner wrote a very popular wedding march, the Bridal Chorus from the opera *Lohengrin*. Lohengrin is a good knight who is given magical powers because he guards the Holy Grail. To help a young maiden, he arrives in a boat drawn by a swan. The swan is actually the young maiden's brother, turned into a swan by evil magic. The story ends with Lohengrin returning to guard the Grail and the swan changing back to the brother.

Today, innocent (and not so innocent) brides walk down the aisle to the organ's majestic "Here comes the bride. . ." The question is, Should a bride use music written by a pagan for an opera based on myth?

> Whatever you do,
> do it all for the glory of God.[33]

If the bride can do it to God's glory, yes. If not, leave it.

> The personal life of the artist is at most a help or a hindrance, but is never essential to his creative task. He may go the way of the Philistine, a good citizen, a fool, or a criminal. His personal career may be interesting and inevitable, but it does not explain his art.[34] (Carl Jung)

The pledge of allegiance of the human artist going it alone might well be:

> In life and painting I can quite well dispense with God. But, suffering as I am, I cannot dispense with something greater than myself, something that is my whole life: the power of creating.[35] (Van Gogh)

The philosophical footing of such an artist might be:

> As non-theists, we begin with humans not God, nature not deity. . . . We can discover no divine purpose or providence for the human species. . . . No deity will save us; we must save ourselves. . . .
> Science affirms that the human species is an emergence from natural evolutionary forces. . . . There is no credible evidence that life survives the death of the body.[36] (*Humanist Manifesto II*)

The *beau geste*, the grand gesture, of the humanistic artist might be to climb to the top of a work of art as Solness the master builder did:

And as I stood up there, high over everything, I said to him: Listen to me, Almighty One! From now on I will be a free Master Builder; free in my sphere, just as you are in yours. I will never more build churches for you; only homes for human beings.[37]

The human artist may want his time on stage alone, without God or Satan present. This may work for a time, but eventually the curtain comes down and a judgment is rendered.[38]

SATANIC ART

But the Devil whoops, as he whooped of old:
"It's clever, but is it Art?"
—Rudyard Kipling[39]

Art is satanic if it is Satan's handiwork or if it shares in Satan's darkness.[40] It is what the black hand of Satan forms through the hand of his artist, the artist Satan has been permitted to test and—if the artist chooses to follow—to forge into an often powerful instrument fit for dark purposes.

Being an artist for the Counterfeiter and Destroyer of life is being rooted in his will, power and plans. Works of the artist who is in league with Satan are marked by

Selfish ambition
Arrogance and boasting
Sexual impurity
Hatred and bitterness
Slander and sarcasm
Cruelty and coldness
Discord
Fits of rage
Piercing noise
Profanity
Blasphemy
No form, chaos
Darkness and depression

68

Emptiness, no answers
Poverty, abandonment and lostness.[41]

Why, then, should the arts celebrate evil? Evil is such a loser! Evil is trying to live down another Year of Defeat—darkness having again failed to put out the light.

Let evil drown its sorrows in its own tears. Let it alone. If evil is going to be celebrated as all-powerful and triumphant, then don't stage it, don't speak it, don't dance it, don't paint it, don't film it.

The artist may deal with evil by putting it into the proper framework: A world-view where
• God is creator, restorer, judge and king.
• Satan is a frustrated, fallen angel.[42] He is tiny and no threat to God, but when seen by even tinier people on earth, he is like a roaring lion.
• People, made by God, rebel and fall. But people can also choose to be restored by God.

There is no true beauty in evil—but plenty of counterfeit glitz. Scratch the surface of Satan's imitation beauty and you will find darkness.

THE CREATIVE PROCESS

Instinct and study; love and hate;
Audacity—reverence. These must mate,
And fuse with Jacob's mystic heart,
To wrestle with the angel—Art.
—Hermann Melville[43]

You are the pen,
But my Spirit does the writing.

In the mystery of this thought which came to me lies the mystery of the creative process. Human hands, human brain, human feet—yet the spirit gives birth to the idea and nurtures the form to have a place on earth. The spirit conceiving the idea and shaping the form may be God, Satan, or human.[44]

> Mozart's essence is not the man himself, but this gift within him, the charisma of sounds, the angel which dictates the music to him. . . . I believe in the angel in Mozart.[45] (Henri Gheon)

Schubert—who could conceive a whole work in his head— was given a poem and asked to set it to music as a serenade. Going to a window, Schubert read it through several times. Turning he said with a smile, "I've got it already, it's done, and it's going to be quite good."[46]

> The creative act, being rooted in the immensity of the unconscious, will forever elude our attempts at understanding. It describes itself only in its manifestations; it can be guessed at, but never wholly grasped.[47] (Jung)

WHAT'S WRONG WITH THE ARTS?

> The arts babblative and scribblative.
> —Robert Southey[48]

> Degrade first the arts if you'd mankind degrade,
> Hire idiots to paint with cold light and hot shade.
> —William Blake[49]

What's wrong with the arts—with theater, dance, painting and film? Simple.

> When the arts withdraw from God,
> God withdraws from the arts.

> When the arts no longer serve God,
> God no longer serves the arts.

> When the arts no longer honor God,
> God no longer honors the arts.

THE GREAT AMERICAN BABY-SITTER

BOB PALMER

SPRINGFIELD (MO) LEADER-PRESS

3-10-75

Why? Because "the earth is the LORD's, and all its full-ness."[50] He *owns* the arts. Because God created the world, he has the right to rule and judge it.[51]

Therefore, when the arts no longer lift a hand in homage to God, God no longer lifts a hand to help the struggling artist, the struggling arts organization. God gives them up.

> They knew all the time that there is a God, yet they refused to acknowledge him as such, or to thank him for what he is or does. Thus they became fatuous in their argumentations, and plunged their silly minds still further into the dark. . . . They gave up God: and therefore God gave them up . . .
>
> These men deliberately forfeited the Truth of God and accepted a lie, paying homage and giving service to the creature instead of to the Creator, who alone is worthy to be worshiped for ever and ever . . .
>
> Moreover, since they considered themselves too high and mighty to acknowledge God, he allowed them to become the slaves of their degenerate minds . . . They became whisperers-behind-doors, stabbers-in-the-dark, God-haters; they overflowed with insolent pride and boastfulness, and their minds teemed with diabolical invention. . . . More than this . . . [they] did not hesitate to give their thorough approval to others who did the same.[52]

So good-by to dark-spirited theater. To foul language. To rancid characters. To downbeat stories. Good-by to look-at-me, ego-stroking dance companies. Good-by to graffiti-mad painters scrawling, "Hey, man, look! I'm not a nobody!"

If the arts want to be on the cutting-edge, then the cutting-edge will have to support the arts. If the arts want to be political, then politics will have to support the arts. If the arts want to court and cater to the devil's disciples, then the devil will bring his spirit and fruit to the theater, to the dance company, to the painter's canvas.

On the other hand, if the arts will serve the world as an ambassador of God, God will then bless the arts. Choose your master well.

THE BEHOLDER

now the eyes of my eyes are opened)
—e. e. cummings[53]

When I consider Your heavens,
  the work of your fingers,
The moon and the stars,
  which You have ordained,
What is man
  that You are mindful of him,
And the son of man
  that You visit him?
—Psalm 8:3–4, new KJV

When a beholder opens himself to a work of art, he opens himself to the spirit which abides in the art. In a work touched by God's love, love flows into the soul of the beholder. The beholder then comes away feeling good, renewed, and uplifted.

When a beholder opens his mind and heart to handiwork having Satan's fingerprints on it, the beholder comes away troubled, depressed, and fearful. Satan, being a deceiver and disguised as an angel of light, may give momentary excitement and pleasure—but it is only momentary. Following the drink is the hangover. Satan's arty disciples and the works of their hands make for a bad brew.

The Italian poet Dante writes of an imagined tour through the gallery of Hell. He looks at a living mural with its starless air and its miserable lot of people who have abandoned hope and who speak in horrible languages. Spiritually lukewarm artists who lived "for themselves" are likely to be among them. Dante's guide tells him, "Speak not of them, but look, and pass them by."[54]

A beholder walking through today's Inferno of Art might do well to listen to the tour guide: "Look once—and pass on."

If a person keeps feeding on rotten art, he keeps feeding the demon that makes the work rotten. To feed on good art is to experience the angel that makes the work good. Further, when a beholder plops money down at the box office, buys a record or a painting, he supports not only the artist but the spirit moving behind the artist.

> We let a work of art act upon us as it acted upon the artist. To grasp its meaning, we must allow it to shape us as it shaped him. Then we also understand the nature of his primordial experience.[55] (Jung)

JUDGING A WORK OF ART TO BE CHRISTIAN

> Dear friends,
> do not believe every spirit,
> but test the spirits
> to see whether they are from God
> —I John 4:1 NIV

Is *Guernica* a Christian Work of Art?

What do we do with a painting in which the bull does not look like a flower-loving Ferdinand? Nor the horse like a circus performer? Nor the lady with a lamp like the Statue of Liberty? Are Christians abandoned and left orphans of modern art?

Not at all. "By their fruit you will recognize them," said Jesus.[56] Just as a tree is good if it bears good fruit, so is a work of art godly if it bears God's fruit, satanic if it bears Satan's fruit, or human art if it bears human fruit. In addition, the Bible gives us a world-view to evaluate earthly creation.

To judge whether a work of art is Christian or not, measure it against the following:

Art is Christian if it reflects a New Testament world-view and bears the fruit of the Holy Spirit.

Forms of art, such as music, that do not have the content to cover a world–view can be judged by the fruit of their spirit alone.

A New Testament World-View	Fruit of the Holy Spirit
• God–in–Christ is creator, re-storer, judge and king.	Love
	Joy
• Satan is the adversary, enemy, destroyer.	Peace
	Patience
• People face to face with God freely rebel or return.	Kindness
	Goodness
	Faithfulness
	Gentleness
	Self-control

"What is the best present-day Protestant religious picture?" Paul Tillich, a theologian interested in art, replied *Guernica*. Guernica is a Spanish town that was bombed and destroyed by German planes in 1937. What Tillich liked in Picasso's painting is that it unmasked, uncovered "the human situation in its depths of estrangement and despair."[57]

Reinhold Niebuhr, a fellow theologian of Tillich's, opposed his friend's position, saying that it was not the whole of Protestantism. Tillich agreed.

> Now this, of course, cannot be the final answer because such a picture is not an affirmative picture. It does not deal with the traditional symbols in any way. It raises the question but does not give the answer. But is it not better to raise the question honestly than to give an answer that is half or totally dishonest because of the traditional bondage?[58]

Let's first look at the painting (p. 75). Although the Germans attacked on a sunny day in spring, the painting is a mural in black, gray and white. The mural is twice as long as high, giving an epic feeling to a close-up viewed by the peasants.[59] Tile is drawn along the bottom of the painting, suggesting a patio or the floor of a Spanish house.[60] In common with a theater set, the scene is both a street scene and the inside of a room.

In the high center of the painting is an oil lamp thrust from a window by a woman who views the carnage on the street in

Pablo Picasso, *Guernica* (1937)

disbelief. She is doing just what Picasso is doing with his brush—seeing and reacting.

The lamp of truth and knowledge en*light*ens the world of the bombing. A ceiling light is merged with the sun; the glare of its bare bulb hides nothing. The newsprint—fresh as the morning paper—is read by a shocked world. The mural is a tabloid and news-real; the urgent story, an exposé.

Also in the center is a horse—part of the animal kingdom that is friendly to people. The horse is screaming. Beneath the horse is the broken body of a fighting man.

On the left side of the painting, a sturdy bull blocks the doorway. His tail is both the smoke of war and the smoke of a volcano having erupted. Brute force like a golden idol rules the day. The bull is unmoved by the agonized cry of a mother holding her dead child.

On the other side of the mural is the other side of the story of rule-by-brawn: A woman falls in terror from a burning building. Peace, loveliness, and innocence are in free fall. Another woman runs like a fugitive. Defenseless women span the barbarian scene.

Nearly all eyes and mouths are toward the bull. Like a Greek chorus in ruins, they scream, "How could you!?" The godlike bull of power stands firm.

There is little hope in the picture. The white bird of peace has a broken wing. The white flower may suggest the peaceful household, farm, and creation that once was, or it may suggest a flower growing as a memorial on the grave of the dead soldier.

What does the painting mean to Picasso?

> The bull is not fascism, but it is brutality and darkness. . . . The horse represents the people.[61]
>
> In *Guernica* I am expressing my horror at the military caste which has plunged Spain into a sea of suffering and death.[62]

Let's evaluate *Guernica* as Christian art.[63] First, the worldview.

- God-in-Christ as creator, restorer, judge and king is absent.
- Satan is vividly painted as the destroyer. Satanic art would cheer. But Picasso's soul cries out in anguish.
- The German people who masterminded the bombing chose to rebel against God's kingdom.

Picasso's protest is not that of a prophet,[64] for a prophet is a messenger who marches from God's realm and never forgets the One whose message he bears. Picasso's cry is more like the cry heard when Herod massacred the innocents.[65] It is raw hurt.

Neither is the painting what Herbert Read imagines:

> It is the modern Calvary, the agony in the bomb-shattered ruins of human tenderness and faith. It is a religious picture . . . inspired. . ."[66]

But not every crucified body is the Christ. The crucified may be a thief or purely human.

In looking for the fruit of the Holy Spirit, we see none. In looking at the fruit of the human spirit, we see concern with earth's freedom, power and peace and what is happening to them. In looking at the destructive fruit of Satan's spirit—so graphically shown—we see it being protested.

Conclusion: *Guernica* is not a Christian work of art but is a work of human art. It protests the lack of peace on earth and man's inhumanity to man. But it leaves out God the restorer, whose judgment came on V-E Day in 1945. It leaves out God the king, who continues to reign triumphantly over his creation called Earth.

CONCLUSION

> Great nations write their autobiographies in three manuscripts—
> the book of their deeds,
> the book of their words,
> and the book of their art.
> —John Ruskin[67]

Over the hills of Hollywood are the familiar letters:
H-O-L-L-Y-W-O-O-D.
But what needs to be written high over the hills of the Silver
Screen, over the Great White Way, over the painter's loft, are
the words:

> Whatsoever things are true,
> Whatsoever things are honest,
> Whatsoever things are just,
> Whatsoever things are pure,
> Whatsoever things are lovely,
> Whatsoever things are of good report;
> If there be any virtue,
> And if there be any praise,
> Think on these things.[68]

Notes

DICTIONARY OF NAMES

Bach (bahK), German organist and composer.

Bouguereau (boo GROW), French painter.

Brunner (BROON er), Swiss Protestant theologian.

Dali (DAH lee), Spanish painter.

Goethe (GER tuh), German poet and dramatist.

Goya (GOY yah), Spanish painter.

Guernica (GWAIR nih kuh: *Spanish* geR NEE kah), a Spanish town.

Haydn (HIGH d'n), Austrian composer.

Jung (yoong), Swiss psychologist and psychiatrist.

Kandinsky (kan KIN skee; *Russian* kun DYEEN skyee), Russian painter.

Klee (clay), Swiss painter.

Niebuhr (NEE boor), United States theologian.

Picasso (peh KAH so), Spanish painter and sculptor in France.

Puccini (poo CHEE nee; *Italian* poot CHEE neh), Italian composer of opera.

Rouault (roo OH), French painter.

Ruskin (RUS kin), English essayist, critic, and social reformer.

Tillich (TILL ick), United States philosopher and theologian, born in Germany.

Van der Leeuw (von der LAY oh), Dutch philosopher and theologian.

Van Gogh (van GOH; *Dutch* vahn KAWK), Dutch painter.

Wagner (VAHG ner), German composer.

—Sources: *The Random House Dictionary of the English Language,* second edition, unabridged, 1987. *Webster's New Collegiate Dictionary,* 1951. *The World Book Encyclopedia,* 1973.

1. John Milton, *Paradise Lost,* VIII, 1. 566.

2. **Other definitions of art**

"United with reason, imagination is the mother of the arts and the source of their wonders."

—Francisco Goya, Spanish painter

"There is only the art of the representation of nature by an artist whose sole aim is to express its truth."

—William Bouguereau, French painter

"The impression and expression of the beautiful we usually call art."

—Gerardus van der Leeuw
Dutch theologian and philosopher

Sources: Robert Goldwater and Marco Treves (compilers and editors), *Artists on Art: From the XIV to the XX Century*, Pantheon Books, 1945, p. 202 for Goya, 288 for Bouguereau.

Gerardus van der Leeuw (preface by Mircea Eliade, translated by David E. Green), *Sacred and Profane Beauty: The Holy in Art*, Holt, Rinehart and Winston, New York, 1963, p. 6.

3. **Vision**
   - 3. the power of perceiving something not actually present to the eye, whether by supernatural insight, imagination, or by clear thinking . . . 4. something seen in the imagination, in a dream, in one's thoughts . . .

     —*The World Book Dictionary*, 1973 Edition
   - "I paint by keeping the eyelids of the tangible world open day and night, closing them from time to time to see the vision flower and take shape."

     —Georges Rouault in G. di San Lazzaro (ed.)
     Homage to Georges Rouault, Tudor Publishing Co., New York, 1971, p. 122

4. Paul Tillich (edited by John Dillenberger and Jane Dillenberger), *On Art and Architecture*, Crossroads, New York, 1987, pp. 231–232.

5. Revelation 8:6 NIV.

6. Revelation 5:11–12 NIV. In the New RSV: "singing with full voice."

7. **God created culture**

   Culture may be thought of as "refined civilization." *Popular culture* is culture that appeals to the *populus*, to the mass of people.

- In the beginning, O Lord,
    you laid the foundations of the earth
            —Hebrews 1:10 NIV
- Now Christ is the visible expression of the invisible God. He existed before creation began, for it was through him that everything was made, whether spiritual or material, seen or unseen. Through him, and for him, also, were created power and dominion, ownership and authority. In fact, every single thing was created through, and for, him. He is both the first principle and the upholding principle of the whole scheme of creation.
            —The Letter to Colossae (Colossians)
            1:15–17 Phillips
- Culture, like marriage and the economic system—and in a certain sense also the State—is based on a spiritual impulse implanted in man's nature, and is thus part of the Divine purpose in creation. We must regard the capacity and the desire for the creation of culture as something which belongs to the primal constituents of the Divine creation of humanity.
            —Emil Brunner (translated by Olive Wyon), *The Divine Imperative*. The Westminster Press, Philadelphia, 1947, p. 484.

8. Genesis 2:19 Amplified. See 1:27.
9. Revelation 14:6.
10. van der Leeuw, p. 74.
11. van der Leeuw, p. 210.
12. van der Leeuw p. 265.
13. **Arts created good**
    Then God saw everything that He had made, and indeed it was very good.
            —Genesis 1:31 New KJV

Fallen:

- We know that the whole creation has been groaning as in the pains of childbirth right up to the present time.
            —Romans 8:22 NIV
- Culture, which in itself is based on the Divine order of creation, is itself also affected by sin, owing to the fact that man,

by his sin, has cut himself off from God. All the culture with which we are familiar owes its origin not only to God but also to sin.

—Brunner, p. 486

14. Bach honestly believed that music was an expression of divinity. He began his scores of sacred music with JJ (*Jesu Juva*, "Jesus, help") and ended with SDG (*Soli Deo Gloria*, "To God alone the Glory").

—Harold C. Schonberg, *The Lives of the Great Composers*, W. W. Norton, New York, 1981, p. 46.

15. Before I formed you in the womb I knew and approved of you [as My chosen instrument], and before you were born I separated and set you apart, consecrating you, and I appointed you a prophet to the nations.

—Jeremiah 1:5 Amplified. See Isaiah 49:1.

16. In Schonberg, p. 401.

17. 2 Samuel 11:2–5,15 and 12:9.

18. John 15:1–8.

19. **The fruit of joy**

"Since God has given me a cheerful heart, He will forgive me for serving him cheerfully."

—Franz Joseph Haydn, composer.
In Schonberg, p. 93.

"Of all the God-gifted dispensers of joy, Johann Strauss is to me the most endearing."

—Richard Strauss (no relation), composer.
In Schonberg, p. 326.

Mozart is one of the greatest religious composers, not primarily because of his church music . . . but because of the reverent joy with which he served his art.

—van der Leeuw, p. 244

20. Galatians 5:22.

21. Revelation 22:19.

22. **The cost of discipleship**

• "I will not sacrifice to the LORD my God burnt offerings that cost me nothing."

—King David, 2 Samuel 24:24 NIV. See Malachi 1:8.

- The moment of inspiration . . . is the pearl for which we have to pay a great price, the price of intense loneliness, the price of that vulnerability which often allows us to be hurt . . .

  —Madeleine L'Engle, *Walking on Water: Reflections on Faith & Art,* Harold Shaw Publishers, Wheaton, Ill., 1980, p. 165.

- Our "Christian shoemaker" must—first of all—do the proper work of a shoemaker. . . . [He] does not differ from another kind of shoemaker simply by the fact that he does the ordinary work of his calling as a service to his neighbour and to the glory of God; rather he will also do "something special" by not always buying in the cheapest and selling in the dearest market . . .

  —Brunner, p. 254, see all of p. 259

23. Not only Handel, but also Bach, used the same music impartially for "spiritual" and "secular" texts.

    —van der Leeuw, p. 220

24. van der Leeuw, pp. 231, 270.

25. John 1:3 KJV. See Colossians 1:15–16 and Hebrews 1:1.

26. John 5:17 Amplified.

27. Dorothy Sayers, *The Mind of the Maker,* Harper & Row, San Francisco, 1941, pp. 37–41.

28. ***Is there Christian art?***

    No

    - There is no Christian art, any more than there is a Christian science.

      —van der Leeuw, p. 279

    - *Christian* art? Art is art; painting is painting; music is music; a story is a story. If it's bad art, it's bad religion, no matter how pious the subject. . . . What is a true icon of God to one person may be blasphemy to another. And it is not possible for us flawed human beings to make absolute, zealous judgments as to what is and what is not religious art.

      —L'Engle, pp. 14,48

    - Old questions of definition are now rendered meaningless. The question, What is Christian art? has no more meaning than what is Christian music, what is Christian literature, what is Christian drama. . . . If a neat answer could be given to either of these questions (What is Christian art? What is religious art?), it might gratify some theologians and logicians, but it would be irrelevant to the artist and to the believer.

—Jane Dillenberger, *Secular Art with Sacred Themes*, Abingdon Press, Nashville, 1969, p. 127

Yes

• Whatever his subject matter, he is a Christian writer if the Christian world view, which is the world view based upon the Bible, is reflected in his writing.

—Frank E. Gaebelein, *The Christian, The Arts, And Truth*, Multnomah, Portland, Oregon, 1985, p. 186.

Gaebelein—GABE uh lin—was a Christian educator and coeditor of *Christianity Today*.

• Faith will be able to make itself felt as a "regulative principle"; hence in this exact and restricted sense it will still be able to produce something like a "Christian" art, science and education, in the same sense in which—which certain reserves—we may speak of Christian marriage . . .

—Brunner, p. 490

29. Alexander Pope, *An Essay on Man*, Epistle II, line 1.

30. Matthew 6:31–33.

31.   In itself, an archetype is neither good nor evil. It is morally neutral, like the gods of antiquity, and becomes good or evil only by contact with the conscious mind, or else a paradoxical mixture of both. Whether it will be conducive to good or evil is determined, knowingly or unknowingly, by the conscious attitude.

—C. G. Jung, *The Spirit in Man, Art, and Literature: Volume 15 of the Collected Works of C. G. Jung*, Pantheon Books, 1966, p. 104 paragraph 160.

32. In Schonberg, pp. 278, 284, 275.

33. **Used for God's glory**

• If I take part in the meal with thankfulness, why am I denounced because of something I thank God for?

So whether you eat or drink or whatever you do, do it all for the glory of God.

—1 Corinthians 10:30–31 NIV

- [In the Reformed Church] everything must and can serve to the glorification of God, even art.
  —van der Leeuw, p. 51

34. Jung, p. 105, paragraph 162.
35. Vincent Van Gogh, quoted in the front matter of Andre Malraux's *The Metamorphosis of the Gods*, Doubleday & Co., Garden City, New York, 1960.
36. *Humanist Manifesto II*, edited by Paul Kurtz, Prometheus Books, Buffalo, New York, 1973, 1984, pp. 16–17.
37. Henrik Ibsen (a new translation by Eva Le Gallienne with a prefatory study), *The Master Builder*, New York University Press, New York, 1955, p. 212.
38. **When the curtain comes down**

    - You have heard, O my soul,
      The sound of the trumpet . . .
      Suddenly my tents are plundered,
      And my curtains in a moment.
      —Jeremiah 4:19–20 new KJV

    - And he told them a parable, saying, "The land of a certain rich man was very productive. . . . And he said, 'This is what I will do: I will tear down my barns and build larger ones . . . And I will say to my soul, "Soul, you have many goods laid up for many years to come; take your ease, eat, drink and be merry." '

      "But God said to him, 'You fool! This very night your soul is required of you; and now who will own what you have prepared?' "
      —Luke 12:16–21 NAS

    - Where there are tongues, they will be stilled.
      —1 Corinthians 13:8 NIV

    - My tent is destroyed,
      And all my ropes are broken;
      My sons have gone from me and are no more.
      There is no one to stretch out my tent again
      Or to set up my curtains.
      —Jeremiah 10:20 NAS

39. Rudyard Kipling, *Ballads and Barrack Room Ballads*, "The Conundrum of the Workshops," st. 6.

40. **Satanic art**
   - Art can be demonic . . . Much art is permeated with a spirit which . . . contradicts everything genuine and pure.
      —van der Leeuw, pp. 278–279
   - Despite Keats' famous line ["Beauty is truth, truth beauty,"], truth is not to be equated with beauty. While in the deepest sense truth is beautiful, because God is absolutely beautiful in his perfection, nevertheless the two—truth and beauty—are not synonymous. The reason is that, although beauty can communicate truth, it can also communicate a lie. Ethically, beauty can be deceptive and downright evil. (The serpent in Eden. Lucifer, an angel of light.) There are various works of art which are decadent and at the same time beautiful; there are those which are corrupt and seductively appealing aesthetically. One does not have to go far to find examples—Baudalaire's *Fleurs de Mal*, Picasso's erotic drawings, many contemporary movies, Jean Genet, a beautiful writer devoted to evil, etc.
      —Gaebelein, p. 47
   - The poet now and then catches sight of the figures that people the night-world—spirits, demons, and gods . . .
      —Jung, p. 95, paragraph 149
41. Many—but not all—come from Galatians 5:19–21 and Romans 1:28–31.
42. **Satan (the Devil)**
   - "Before man fell the devil fell. The devil is, in fact, a fallen angel. His sin and fall consists in his effort to transcend his proper state and to become like God."
      —Reinhold Niebuhr, *Nature and Destiny of Man*, Charles Scribner's Sons, New York, 1946, p. 180.
   - Satan with his fellow angels flung out of heaven (Revelation 12:7–9 and Luke 10:17–18) and his only power being what God delegates to him (Luke 4:5–6 and Job 1:12).
   - "Your enemy the devil prowls around like a roaring lion looking for someone to devour." (1 Peter 5:8 NIV)
43. Hermann Melville, *Timoleon*, Art.

44. The creative spirit

- A certain fire, an impulse to create, is kindled, is transmitted through the hand, leaps to the canvas, and in the form of a spark leaps back to its starting place, completing the circle—back to the eye and further (back to the source of the movement, the will, the idea).

  —Paul Klee, *Paul Klee: Watercolors, Drawings, Writings*, Verlag M. DuMont Schauberg, Cologne, Germany, 1969, pp. 7,8.

- [In a true artist] the voice of the soul will in some degree make itself heard. . . . The inner voice tells him what form he needs, whether inside or outside nature.

  —Wassily Kandinsky, *Concerning the Spiritual in Art: and painting in particular, 1912*, George Wittenborn, New York, 1955, pp. 74–75.

- [The artist] would present to the world a whole, yet this whole he cannot find in nature. It is a product of his own spirit, or, if you like, of a divine spirit.

  —Goethe, in *Goethe* by Karl Heinemann. Quoted in Kandinsky, p. 73.

- [Another type of artist] is overwhelmed by a flood of thoughts and images which he never intended to create and which his own will could never have brought into being. . . . He is aware that he is subordinate to his work or stands outside it, as though he were a second person; or as though a person other than himself had fallen within the magic circle of an alien will.

  —Jung, p. 73, paragraph 110.

45. Henri Gheon, *In Search of Mozart*, New York, 1934. Quoted in van der Leeuw, p. 244.

46. In Schonberg, p. 131.

47. Jung, p. 97, paragraph 135.

48. Robert Southey, *Colloquies on the Progress and Prospects of Society*, no. 1, pt. 2.

49. William Blake, *Annotations to Sir Joshua Reynolds's Discourses*, title page. Vol. I of Reynolds's *Works*, edited by Edmond Malone, 2nd edition, 1798.

50. Psalm 24:1 New KJV.
51. A clearly-written, theological evaluation of the outlook presented in these pages may be found in H. Richard Niebuhr's *Christ and Culture,* Harper & Brothers, New York, 1951, Chapter 6, "Christ Transformer of Culture." Part I, pp. 190–196, is Niebuhr's summary and evaluation, and Part II, pp. 196–206, a Biblical basis for the position as found in The Gospel According to John. Sample:

    > The conversionist, with his view of history as the present encounter with God in Christ, does not live so much in expectation of a final ending of the world of creation and culture as in awareness of the power of the Lord to transform all things by lifting them up to himself. (p. 195)

52. The Letter to Rome (Romans) 1:21–25, 28–32 Phillips.
53. The line from "i thank You God for most this amazing," is reprinted from COMPLETE POEMS, 1904–1962, by E. E. Cummings, Edited by George J. Firmage, by permission of Liveright Publishing Corporation. Copyright (c) 1950, 1978, 1991 by the Trustees for the E. E. Cummings Trust.
54. Dante (translated by Henry F. Cary with complete notes and illustrated by Gustave Dore), *The Divine Comedy of Dante Alighieri: Inferno, Purgatory, Paradise,* Crown Publishers, New York, no date, "Hell," Canto III, p. 20.
55. Jung, p. 105, paragraph 161.
56. **Judging spiritually**
    - Thus, by their fruit you will recognize them.
      —Matthew 7:20 NIV
    - [A work of art] has power to create spiritual atmosphere; and from this internal standpoint alone can one judge whether it is a good work of art or bad. If its form is "poor," it is too weak to call forth spiritual vibration. . . . [A picture] is only well painted if its spiritual value is completed and satisfying.
      —Kandinsky p. 74
57. Tillich, pp. 95–96.
58. Tillich, p. 191.

59. Rudolf Arnheim, *Picasso's Guernica, The Genesis of a Painting*, University of California Press, Berkeley, 1962, pp. 20, 26.
60. Herschel B. Chipps, *Picasso's Guernica*, University of California Press, Berkeley, 1988, p. 134.
61. Lael Wertenbaker and the Editors of TIME-LIFE BOOKS, *The World of Picasso 1880*—New York, 1967, p. 127. The book has a large foldout of *Guernica*.
62. Denis Thomas, *Picasso and His Art*, Book Value International, Northbrook, Illinois, 1981, p. 67.
63. **Judging art: Is it Christian?**
    Tillich comments on a number of paintings. While he evaluates them in terms of people's *ultimate concern for Ultimate Reality* (by which he means "religious" p. 232) I will comment on them in terms of *world-view* and *fruit*.

    The Sacrament of the Last Supper by Salvador Dali. (Picture on p. 90) Tillich referred to the figure of Jesus Christ in the painting as:

    > a sentimental but very good athlete in an American baseball team. . . . The technique is a beautifying naturalism of the worst kind. I am horrified by it. [It is] simply junk. (Tillich, p. xvi)

    The painting shows the last supper in a modern setting. Jesus is looking ahead and up to the Father. The path to the Father is through the crucified body, high and lifted up, which embraces Jesus, the disciples, and the world. "And I, when I am lifted up from the earth, will draw all people to myself." (John 12:32 New RSV)

    The disciples kneel reverently before the holy mystery. Light from heaven—from the Father and angels unseen—glows. There is no fruit of Satan in this painting, as in other works of Dali. The fruit that stands out is love, patience, goodness and faithfulness.

    Now about Jesus being an all-American . . . The songwriter sings that "Some Children See Him" as "lily-white," with long hair "soft and fair." Some children see him as

Salvador Dali, *The Sacrament of the Last Supper* (1955)

"almond-eyed," with a skin coloring of "yellow." Still others see him as "bronzed" or "dark," even as they are.* The universal Christ who is above race and culture appears to each particular race in their own color, culture and tongue. Conclusion: an authentic, Christian painting.

Christ Mocked by Soldiers by Georges Rouault. (Picture on p. 92) While "authentic," Tillich feels it "does not succeed" completely in trying to present a solution to the human predicament. (pp. 232–233,99) What Tillich likes are the two mocking soldiers:

> The two mocking soldiers are better than the Christ. . . . It is possible, even out of the evil of these two horrible faces, to make a great and beautiful picture. (p. 109)

The painting—influenced by stained-glass art—shows the body of Jesus Christ, head bowed, eyes closed. Off to the sides are two clownlike soldiers, mocking.

The focus of Rouault's painting, rightly, is the figure of Jesus Christ, not the two off-center soldiers. Jesus reflects the fruit of peace in accepting the Father's plan of the cross. He shows the fruit of love, the deep love that would bear up under humiliation and the cross—and mocking soldiers. Conclusion: a Christian painting.

Animals in a Landscape (Painting with Bulls II) by Franz Marc. (Picture on p. 94) Tillich writes:

> It is indeed possible to see . . . the immediate revelation of an absolute reality in the relative things; the depth-content of the world, experienced in the artist's religious ecstasy, shines through the things; they have become "sacred" objects. (p. 54)

The modern painting shows two oxen and a cow at peace in a landscape. What "shines through the things" is the hand of the Creator and his Spirit moving. (Genesis 1:1,2 Amplified) Take away the Creator's hand and Spirit and you are left with human art.

---

*"Some Children See Him." Lyric by Wihla Hutson. Music by Alfred Burt. Hollis Music, New York, 1954 and 1967.

Georges Rouault, *Christ Mocked by Soldiers* (1932)

The painting captures God's act of creating, a world-view from Genesis not Darwin. The painting suggests animals were created as they look today, not creatures clawing their way out of a swamp. The fruit of the Holy Spirit that seems to stand out is the love and joy of the creative act and the peace of the animals. Conclusion: a Christian painting.

64. Tillich finds "prophetic wrath" in *Guernica*. Tillich, p. 179.
65. Anthony Blunt, *Picasso's "Guernica,"* Oxford University Press, 1969, p. 44.
66. "Herbert Read Guernica: A Modern Calvary," in Ellen C. Oppler (ed.), *Picasso's Guernica*, W. W. Norton & Co., New York, 1988, p. 218.

    Herbert Read was a magazine editor, taught art history at the university level, and published writings on art history, literary criticism, and poetry.

67. John Ruskin, *St. Mark's Rest*, preface.
68. Philippians 4:8 KJV.

Franz Marc, *Animals in a Landscape* (1914)

He redeemed my soul from going
down to the pit,
and I will live to enjoy the light.
—Job 33:28 NIV

Alice in . . . Censored!

YOUNG Alice[1] was walking the hills outside of San Francisco. Her walk quickened as she saw the April clouds darken. A few drops of rain spattered her blue dress and streaked her white bib apron. "Time to run," she thought girlishly. "Time to find a rabbit hole!"

As she ran, her long blond hair blew in the swelling wind. Seeing a white rabbit hop into his hole, Alice thought, "I'll follow him!" Whether young Alice shrank in size or the rabbit hole wondrously enlarged, Alice didn't know. All she knew is she jumped into the hole.

DOWN . . . Down . . . down . . . down. THUMP! She landed unhurt on a pile of dry leaves and grass. "How could *down* . . . be so bright?" she puzzled, looking around. Then she heard a gifted sound, which helped lift her gently to her feet. "What beautiful music," she said aloud. "What beautiful words!"

Enchanted, Alice followed the sound. Peeking through a red rose-tree, she saw the top of a hill, which was circled by soft clouds. "A view of heaven," she muttered mystically. "Yet—how very queer. How can heaven be down?"

There on the hill was a caterpillar with the loveliest markings and colors Alice had ever seen—almost too beautiful. He was playing a lyre while speaking lines of high drama. "A caterpillar who's a musician . . . an actor . . . a writer!" laughed Alice delightfully. She ran up the grassy hill to greet the creative caterpillar. "Good day, Mr. Caterpillar!"

"Bad day to you, too." He resumed playing his small harp and writing down the dialogue he spoke.

"Bad day?" puzzled Alice aloud. "But why?"

Twisting his face into an ugly contortion, he sneered out the reason. "*Censors*. They will not let me create the art I want."

"How unfair!" protested Alice. "I can tell you're an artist. And a good one!"

"A great one. And yet . . . persecuted." With a melancholy spirit, the persecuted caterpillar began reciting words, beautiful words. What did they mean? Alice wasn't sure—but they were beautiful, make no mistake.

"Jealousy. I bet it's jealousy," spoke up Alice with an emphatic nod of the head. "Others write the same ol' sameness . . . much of a muchness. But not you!"

"From my new play—which those in power will not let me produce." Angrily, the put-upon caterpillar tossed his small harp aside.

"How unfair!" repeated Alice. "How dare they!" Alice's young liberal heart was cut to the quick by the news.

"He who holds the purse strings holds the curtain from going up."

"Stuff and nonsense! Who do they think they are?" smoldered Alice.

"Judges."

"JUDGES! Fiddle-de-dee! Who made *them* judges! Why aren't *you* the judge? Why am *I* not the judge!? Judges," scoffed Alice, upset.

"Will you . . . judge my play?" inquired the poor caterpillar.

"Of course."

The caterpillar brightened, a glint darting from his eye. "Will you . . . play a role in it?"

"Certainly."

"At last! I have found a seeker after truth!"

"Down to my bones I believe in truth."

"You won't let me down . . . like the—" The castigated caterpillar twisted his face again into a distortion as he uttered the hated word: "—censors."

"NEVER!" said Alice boldly. She'd rather die than let truth die.

"You'll see it through . . . to the end?"

"Of course."

"Good!" chirped the caterpillar, having gotten Alice to commit herself.

"What is your play about?" asked Alice innocently.

"Sadomasochism and homoeroticism . . . necrophilia . . . incest and cannibalism. In short, truth—the truth no one wants to look at."[2]

Alice's mouth fell open. "Really!" She gulped. She didn't know what most of those words meant, but she did believe in artistic freedom . . . like protest marches for "Save the Caterpillar." Now *that* she could understand.

"Act one, scene one," announced the caterpillar simply. He knew the script by memory. "Stand there among the daisies." Alice hurried over, eager to support artistic expression. "Now hold out your arms and turn like a flower blowing in the breeze. That's it. You're free! Completely f-r-e-e . . ."

Alice laughed gaily. "It's fun! I like your play!"

"Good. Now unbutton your dress."

Alice stopped. "What?"

"Unbutton your dress. Clothes inhibit movement. Your body is crying to be free, Alice. Free it from its chain of rags!"

"But . . . I don't hear it crying," replied Alice, artlessly.

"*I* hear it. Your body is in torment," cried out the caterpillar dramatically.

"Dear me. I'm afraid . . . I'm not used to that," explained Alice chastely.

"You have been brainwashed . . . taught to deny your body. But I say 'Love your body! Set it free!' "

"Maybe . . . we can go on to the next page," brightly suggested Alice.

"As you like," sighed the caterpillar, momentarily deflated. "In the play, after you slip off your dress, wave it in the air and toss it to the wind—right into the face of the censors! See how they like that!"

"And then?"

"Then . . . your lace dainties."

"SIR! Mind yourself!"

"You do it every day. Why not in my play?"

"NOT ON STAGE I DON'T!"

"What I write has artistic merit. It is essential to the play. Come, come, slip them off."

"I—I—" Nothing else came. Alice stood rigidly . . . silently . . . and fully dressed.

"You're not . . . one of *them*, are you?" slyly inquired the caterpillar with a faint smile.

"Me?! A BLUE PENCILER!?"

The caterpillar screwed his mouth, pausing. He looked at Alice questioningly. "You do believe in my play, don't you?"

"I—" Alice swallowed hard. "I believe in your play and that you have a right to see it staged. But I tell you again: Go on to the next page."

The clever caterpillar smiled at her renewed commitment. He beckoned toward a tree. From behind the tree came a nude boy. "Scene two. The love scene."

Alice took one look at the *au naturel* boy and quickly looked away. "Scene three, please."

"As you like." He sang out a clear tone, which brought two giggly, but-oh-so-naked girls from behind a bush. "The four of you—all make love! Explore the nature of love. Express yourselves! Be free. Free! FREE!"

The three children in their birthday suits ran toward Alice.

"*Don't touch me!*" said Alice flatly. "Not . . . just now." Whew! she thought to herself, my escapes are getting more and more narrow. Yet I will not be numbered among the scissor-people! Artists *must* be free to tell the truth. "Censorship is evil," she whispered to give herself courage. "Censorship is evil. Censorship is—"

"Perhaps scene four?" asked the crafty caterpillar. The caterpillar began speaking exquisite words as he walked in a circle. Then a gust of wind snapped a thin branch from a tree and mysteriously carried the branch to Alice, letting it fall at her feet.

"Curiouser and curiouser," remarked Alice, picking up the branch—and relieved it wasn't a naked body falling from the tree like an apple.

"To make your body tingle. Your flesh will never feel more alive than when you s-t-r-o-k-e it with the branch. Like this," demonstrated the caterpillar, holding an imaginary stick.

"A WHIP! *Me?* Whip my back?!" Alice was anguished.

"Please, Alice," patiently explained the artistic caterpillar. "I'm revealing life to you. By the time you finish doing my play, you will know good and evil." His eyes flashed as he approached her. "Trust me, my young innocent. I know much."

Alice shivered. Was it the weather? But the day was warm. Was it his eye? It seemed to stare right through her. Was it his voice? It seemed to echo from another world. Or was it the way he moved toward her without stepping, just . . . floating?

"My sweet. *I* will do it for you." The grinning caterpillar raised the branch.

Horrified, Alice shouted at her outlawed writer. "*Don't you dare!* Get to the ending of your play!"

Giggling, the cast of two girls and a boy ran up to Alice. While the girls held Alice's hands, the boy wrapped a vine around Alice's neck. Around . . . around . . . around.

"Stop it . . . you're choking me. . ."

"What is the end of anything—but death." The caterpillar surveyed the sky, the clouds. "The greater the art, the greater the death. Of deathless art, I AM MASTER! I rule! *I rule!*"

"He rules," chorused the rehearsed children. "Our master builder rules!"

"Dear God, help me," breathed Alice, beginning to lose strength and consciousness.

"Baa. Baa." It was a lamb skipping forth from the thicket.[3]

"Go away from me!" screamed the caterpillar at the lamb. "Get away!" He began backstepping. "Don't come near me!" But the lamb kept prancing toward him. "Baa. Baa."

"NOOOOOOOOOOO . . . . . I know who you are!"[4]

The children actresses and actor released Alice and ran to hiding places. Alice, reviving, then saw a most remarkable thing. A black spirit, shaped like an eel and with one big eye in his head, came out of the caterpillar with a shriek. The caterpillar was thrown to the ground, his many-splendored skin crumpling like an old rag.[5] The black spirit was a thinking spirit, one who used knowledge to deceive.

"A demon," spoke Alice aloud. "The artist who looked so beautiful and spoke so beautifully . . . The artist who was a law to himself . . . he housed a demon spirit!" Alice was astonished. "The artist who spoke of freedom with no boundaries . . . a serpent!" Alice looked and saw the girl and boy playactors hiding from the lamb.

Feeling the weight of testings lift from her, Alice sighed. "I feel lighter. Yet I've got to get out of here. But how?"

"Baa," nodded the lamb, indicating with his head the way of escape.

With a heart full of thanksgiving, Alice hurried back toward the rabbit hole. "But how," she wondered, "how could something so beautiful be so weird?" Other thoughts tumbled through her mind. "Boundaries. Then . . . they're not to keep us from growing, but to keep us safe. And censorship . . . I guess it can be either good or bad—depending in whose hands it is. In God's hands, it's terrific—it keeps the demons in their cages.[6] And without it—" Pausing, Alice looked back. "The bottom of a rabbit hole . . . can be hell."

Alice found her path and hurried along. "Knowledge . . . I already know what is good. I don't need a looney caterpillar to show me. What he was showing me beyond the boundaries was flat out *evil!* Death! Dear God," exclaimed Alice, her head expanding with knowledge far beyond her years. "Thank you for bringing me back."

Alice arrived at the rabbit hole. Darting in, she began climbing up. "Now I know why *heaven* was down. It wasn't heaven at all! And the truth nobody wanted to look at . . . why it wasn't truth at all, but evil." Alice shook her head. "And *Be free! Be free!* . . . nothing but a temptation. The only real thing," she thought climbing up, "was the ending: death. Wow! That was close!"

Alice reached the top of the rabbit hole and peeked out. The rain had ended. The sun—the real sun—was shining. "It's good to be home. . ." She reached to pick a dandelion, adding, "Boundaries and all."[7]

Notes

1. Lewis Carroll, *Alice's Adventures in Wonderland,* Macmillan, 1865. *Through the Looking-Glass, and What Alice Found There,* Macmillan, 1871. The illustration is a detail from the original drawings of John Tenniel.

2. **Definitions**

   Definitions—but not pronunciations—are from Webster's *Third New International Dictionary,* except where otherwise noted.

   Sadomasochism (Say' doe MAS uh kiz m). A form of perversion marked by a love for both receiving and inflicting pain. (*The World Book Dictionary*)

   Homoeroticism (Hoe' moe eh ROT uh ciz m). Homosexuality. 2. erotic activity with a member of one's own sex.

   Necrophilia (Nek' row FILL ee uh). Fascination with the dead; *specifically:* obsession with and usually erotic attraction toward and stimulation by corpses . . .

Evil outside of truth

An artist can show the reality of evil, but he cannot show others "the truth in evil" because there is no truth in evil. "I am the way, the truth, and the life," said Jesus. (John 14:6 New KJV) He did NOT say, "I am the lost way. I am evil. I am death." The Evil One "does not stand in the truth, because there is no truth in him." (John 8:44) Evil is outside of truth.

What is truth

Truth is "the rational structure that gives meaning to the universe." (A definition given for *logos,* "Word," as found in John 1:1. Source unknown.) Evil steals, kills, and destroys (John 10:10), which is why it is not "rational" and why it does not give "meaning" to life. Evil is outside the realm of truth—which is a good reason to have nothing to do with it.

  • How can light fellowship with darkness? What harmony can there be between Christ and Belial [the devil]? Or what has a believer in common with an unbeliever?
  —2 Corinthians 6:14,15 Amplified

- But test and prove all things [until you can recognize] what is good; [to that] hold fast. Abstain from evil—shrink from it and keep aloof from it—in whatever form or whatever kind it may be.

  —1 Thessalonians 5:21,22 Amplified

3. The story of the lamb

- Abraham answered, "God himself will provide the lamb . . ."

  —Genesis 22:8 NIV

- The next day John saw Jesus coming toward him and said, "Look, the Lamb of God, who takes away the sin of the world!"

  —John 1:29 NIV

- "They will make war against the Lamb, but the Lamb will overcome them because he is Lord of lords and King of kings—and with him will be his called, chosen and faithful followers."

  —Revelation 17:14 NIV

4.   In the synagogue there was a man possessed by a demon, an evil spirit. He cried out at the top of his voice, "Ha! What do you want with us, Jesus of Nazareth? Have you come to destroy us? I know who you are—the Holy One of God!"

"Be quiet!" Jesus said sternly. "Come out of him!" Then the demon threw the man down before them all and came out without injuring him.

All the people were amazed . . .

—Luke 4:33–36a NIV

5. Lucifer

- How you are fallen from heaven,
  O Lucifer!

  —Isaiah 14:12 Smith-Goodspeed

- You said in your heart,
  "I will ascend above the tops of the clouds;
    I will make myself like the Most High."
  But you are brought down to the grave,
    to the depths of the pit.
  All your pomp has been brought down to the grave,
    along with the noise of your harps.

  —Isaiah 14:13a,14,15,11a NIV

- You were puffed up with pride through your beauty,
  you ruined your wisdom by reason of your splendor;
  therefore I flung you to the ground, and exposed you . . .
  —Ezekiel 28:17 Smith-Goodspeed

6. Censorship

Definition: **censor** 2. a person who tells others how they ought to behave; a person who exercises supervision over the morals or behavior of others. (*The World Book Dictionary*)

Life on earth began with censorship.

"From every tree in the garden you are free to eat; but from the tree of the knowledge of good and evil you must not eat . . ."
—Genesis 2:16,17 Smith-Goodspeed

Civilization continued with censorship:

You shall have no other gods before me.

You shall not misuse the name of the LORD your God.

You shall not covet your neighbor's wife.
—Exodus 20:3,7a,17b, NIV

Censorship is a sign reading, "No Trespassing." If God puts up the sign, all is well. If humans put up the sign, it may or may not be well. If Satan puts up the sign, it is to block out knowledge and holiness.

Censorship is a form of government. Government is good. To abolish censorship is to abolish government. On earth, someone is going to rule. Will it be those of good will—or the rebels, the lawless ones?

7. Civil boundaries

Hard-core material is obscene and not protected by the First Amendment when, taken as a whole, the average person using prevailing community standards finds 1) it appeals to the prurient interest in sex, and 2) sexual acts are portrayed in a patently offensive way, and 3) the material has no serious literary, artistic, political, or scientific value.

—(*Miller* v. *California*, 1973)

Civil judges

Who, using the above three-part test, decides what is obscene? Not the artist and not his peddler. The courts and those who govern, the agents of the people decide.

Civil protection

The Court ruled material cannot be banned because it "advocates an idea," and, defending privacy, ruled:

> If the First Amendment means anything, it means that a State has no business telling a man, sitting alone in his own house, what books he may read or what films he may watch. Our whole constitutional heritage rebels at the thought of giving government the power to control men's minds.

> —"Idea" in *Kingsley Picture Corp.* v. *Regents*, 1959, and "privacy" in *Stanley* v. *Georgia*, 1969. In Daniel S. Moretti, *Obscenity and Pornography: The Law Under the First Amendment*, Oceana Publications, Inc. New York, 1984, pp. 22–23 for *Kingsley*, 26–27 for *Stanley*, 30–34 for *Miller*.)

Key thoughts (all in *Paris Adult Theatre I* v. *Slaton*, 1973)
Chief Justice Berger:

> The fantasies of a drug addict are his own and beyond the reach of government, but government regulation of drug sales is not prohibited by the Constitution.

> —In *The Supreme Court Obscenity Decisions: The complete text of the decisions of June 21, 1973*, Greenleaf Classics, Inc., San Diego, 1973, p. 40.

Mr. Justice Brennan (dissent):

> I would hold, therefore, that at least in the absence of distribution to juveniles or obtrusive exposure to unconsenting adults, the First and Fourteenth Amendments prohibit the state and federal governments from attempting wholly to suppress sexually oriented materials on the basis of their allegedly "obscene" contents. Nothing in this approach precludes those governments from taking action to serve what may be strong and legitimate interests through regulation of the manner of distribution of sexually oriented material.

> —In *Decisions*, p. 88

Chief Justice Burger:

> Although most pornography may be bought by elders, "the heavy users and most highly exposed people to pornography are adolescent females (among women) and adolescent and

BOB SULLIVAN
Courtesy Worcester (Mass.) Telegram

Death of a Salesman

young males (among men)." The Report of the Commission on Obscenity (1970 ed.), 401. The legitimate interest in preventing exposure of juveniles to obscene materials cannot be fully served by simply barring juveniles from the immediate physical premises of "adult" bookstores, when there is a flourishing "outside business" in these materials.

> —In *Decisions*, p. 30

As Chief Justice Warren stated there is a "right of the Nation and of the States to maintain a decent society . . ."

> —In *Decisions*, p. 32

Professor Alexander Bickel, a constitutional scholar;

> It concerns the tone of the society . . . the style and quality of life, now and in the future. A man may be entitled to read an obscene book in his room, or expose himself indecently there . . . . We should protect his privacy. But if he demands a right to obtain the books and pictures he wants in the market, and to foregather in public places—discreet, if you will, but accessible to all—with others who share his tastes, then to grant him his right is to affect the world about the rest of us, and to impinge on other privacies. Even supposing that each of us can, if he wishes, effectively avert the eye and stop the ear (which, in truth, we cannot), what is commonly read and seen and heard and done intrudes upon us all, want it or not.

> —Quoted by Burger in *Decisions*, pp. 31–32

When liberties collide

When an artist, rock singer, filmmaker, speaker, printer or worshiper leaves the privacy of his room and enters the market place where his liberties may "collide with the liberties of others," he enters into "Caesar's affairs and may be regulated by the state." Freedom is not absolute; freedom has boundaries.

> —See *Prince* v. *Massachusetts*, 1944. Justice Jackson in dissent. George W. Spicer, *The Supreme Court and Fundamental Freedoms*, Appleton-Century-Crofts, New York, 1959, pp. 70–71.
>
> See Romans 13:1–7. Titus 3:1. 1 Peter 2:13–17.

Putting the blame on porn

"Porn made me do it," complains the man who batters, rapes and snuffs out women. But one man's fantasy is another man's yawn. The problem is not with the porn but with the man.

The-devil-made-me-do-it is a weak argument. Satan is permitted to test people, but he is limited to tests that are 1) common to every person on this earth. 2) Never more than a person can bear. 3) Always with a way out provided by God. (I Corinthians 10:13)

Yes, Satan can work through soft and hard porn. (He has even been known to work through television evangelists.) But taking away Satan's arsenal of the hard-core obscene is enough for courts of law. When a criminal points his finger at girlie shows and cries, "That serpent made me do it!" he has three fingers pointing back at him—the real culprit. The guilt rests with the man who says yes to Satan—and then does the deed with his own hands.

—See *Time*, March 30, 1992, pp. 52–53.

A parable on funding the arts

Once in a nearby land, a small classical dance company was awarded $50,000, which nicely filled their slippers-in-hand. A modern painter was awarded $20,000, which he stuffed into the upturned beret he held. A novelist, waiting to be inspired before beginning his great work, received $10,000.

The awards were based on the recipients' talents and past performances. For these reasons, the sums were different.

After a time, the artists reported to the award-giver, who "settled accounts with them." Two recipients heard, "Well done!" The "wicked and lazy" third recipient heard, "Throw the good-for-nothing out!"

This parable is a modern version of The Parable of the Talents. (Matthew 25:14–30) The parable told by Jesus is a guide for funding artists—and doing it with accountability.

The story shows in the end that no blank check, no do-your-own-thing is ever given by the master of funding arts.

In its mission statement, the National Endowment for the Arts says, "It must not . . . direct artistic content." That's fine. But the NEA also needs to add, "It must not . . . play the fool by funding the foolish."

In funding artists, the National Endowment for the Arts should fund *projects,* not artists per se. Artistic talent and past performances would still be considered, but carte blanche would be eliminated. (For do-your-own-thing art, private funds may be tapped.)

An artistic project should show a clear benefit to the American people, to American culture. The project may benefit America as a whole, in region, or in part. The project may be future, current, or recently completed. It may be original or an adaptation. It may or may not be commercial.

The truth of the Parable of the Talents is that whatever our gifts, we are held accountable for them.

When the woman saw
    that it was a delight to the eyes
    and was to be desired to make one wise,
She ate.

          —Genesis 3:6
            based on New RSV, condensed

Me, Jane

IT WAS nice in the beginning. Jane, Man and Boy knew peace and laughter. They lived in the wilds of Florida, in a secluded area tucked between Big Cypress Swamp and the Everglades. "Eden" they called it.[1]

Man ruled the wilds with wisdom and kindness, collecting fresh fruit from high in the trees and bringing home fresh milk from animals. Eden was like a preserve, parrots squawking, alligators sunning, and flamingos standing on one leg. Man viewed his role in Eden as "keeper of the garden." An old missionary's Bible was all he had to go on.

Jane, his wife, radiated love and nurture, creating an invisible womb around Eden. This was her unique role. Jane felt safe and loved with Man. She found a completeness with Man and Boy, like a completed circle. They called it "family."

While Man was particularly good at swinging through the trees picking oranges and mangoes, Jane was better at finding strawberries and wild vegetables. So several times a week Jane was the food-gatherer and Man stayed home, and while at home he would teach, work, play sports and fish with Boy. They felt this form of family was right for them and felt God's blessing upon it, leaving the family more closely drawn to their Creator and to each other.

Jane always knew when Man was returning home. She would hear his greeting ring through the trees as he came swinging from vine to vine. "OH-oh-OH-oh-OH-oh-O-O-O-O-O-O-O-H! . . . ."

Jane would bathe daily in a pool, and afterwards she would lie in the sun to dry off. One sunny day as Jane was bathing, a waterproof knapsack came floating down the stream that led into the pool. Curious, Jane pulled it ashore and looked inside. There was a magazine called *Trespass: A Journal of Enlightenment*. It was news from the outside world! Jane's eyes widened.

"You can have it all!" proclaimed the cover story.

"I never thought of that," mumbled Jane. "Here I can roam anywhere I want to—except east of Eden." It was there God placed a *No Trespassing* sign.

"What's this?" Jane pulled out a mirror with its corner broken off. Looking in the mirror, she was struck with awe. "It's me! And I'm beautiful. . ."

Carefully placing the mirror aside so she could take it home with her, Jane turned to an article in the magazine. Her eyes again widened.

> One man—how primitive. How utterly BORING! Don't you women know what you're missing? Different sensibilities, different auras, different awakenings. PLEASE! Don't limit yourself to one man!

Jane felt her cheeks flush. She looked around, feeling someone . . . something . . . might be watching. Hurrying to a tree, she buried her magazine safely beneath some leaves and branches. No one would find it there.

The next morning Jane quickly arose from her bed and ran to uncover her magazine. Brushing off the leaves, her eyes again widened as she read:

All you wonderful, wild, untamed women out there—why limit yourself to *men?* The female body is beautiful! And how do you know "lavender" isn't your color unless you wear it? Remember, "Feminism is the theory, and lesbianism is the practice."[2]

Write to us about your affair—whichever way you swing. Take the plunge. S-t-r-e-t-c-h! You owe it to yourself to be and enjoy the best! Sex is recreation. Sex is fulfilling. Sex is for YOU!

"I've settled for less," muttered Jane, slapping the magazine to the ground. "I've given my best years to one man. Years . . . *wasted!*" With growing resentment, Jane began pacing. Drawn to the magazine, she picked it up again and turned to the next article.

Are you still making porridge for your Papa Bear? Well, Goldilocks, get with it. Take the porridge, dump it on the head of your bearish husband, and split! (TIP: Don't forget your hairbrush. You want to look good for that someone "special" in your life!)

There's a whole world of jobs out there waiting for that chic, sophisticated Goldilocks who can put it all together with sensitivity and style. Men are so clumsy! Why should *they* be lawyers, executives, and corporation presidents? Look in the mirror. Who is more capable than you? Go for it! You deserve it.

"How lucky," said Jane, seeing things for the first time and clutching the magazine to her heart. "How lucky to have women show me the way. But look at me, here, living in a stupid hut in a stupid swamp! Well, Big Daddy, it's bye-bye. Little Jane's going to cross the road!"[3]

Early the next morning, Jane quietly arose. She slipped into a jumpsuit that was hand-stitched, form-fitting, and panther black. Dipping her finger into red berry juice, she wrote on her broken mirror: *Me, Jane.* With that she left.

Jane made her way to the boundary of Eden, the eastern edge. She looked around, wondering if she might have been followed. By whom? Creatures, spirits . . . who knows? Going to the *No Trespassing* sign, she pulled it from the ground and tossed it aside. It landed in a puddle. Jane watched it for a moment as part of it sank in the mud. She knew she had turned Eden's world topsy-turvy—no longer was it God-Husband-Jane[4] but Jane-Husband-God.

"I'm sorry, God," Jane said sadly. "But it has to be this way. I feel I owe it to you to say why I'm leaving. First, there's this male thing. I know the old missionary's Bible says you're spirit and not male or female,[5] but my magazine says you're male. Who am I to believe?!

"Another reason I'm leaving is that Eden isn't big enough for both of us. Either you rule or I rule. The old missionary's Bible says you are love and all love comes from you.[6] I know this because I've experienced it. But I simply will not submit to a Spirit of Love. Not when I can rule myself and become the woman I choose to be! And there's more.

"You want me to have one man. I want many. You created me from Adam's rib so I would always be a part of him.[7] How unfair! A woman's body is beautiful! I want to make love to women, too, don't you see?

"You made me to give birth. I may choose to abort. You want me to love and nurture my children. I want the Child Care Center to raise them. You want me to submit to a godly husband.[8] I want him to submit to me! You want me to give you a tithe. My magazine says I should give my tithe to feminist causes.[9] You want me to study the old missionary's Bible with Man, but I want to join a CR group to raise my consciousness, to raise my voice, and to tell them how oppressed I am![10]

"You want me to worship you alone. Well, I'm fed up with a jealous god! I want to worship a Mother Goddess with a womb and breasts. If you don't lighten up, you won't have anyone around to listen to you! Your commandments written on stone should have been written on sand so you could update them.

"SO WHAT IF I HAVE AN ABORTION, ADAM,... WHO'LL EVER KNOW?"

Your days of thunder and lightning are through! Mt. Sinai is . . . extinct!"

Jane felt she may have put a chink in God's china, so she added respectfully, "I'm sorry to be so blunt. But you see, it's not that you're male—it's that you rule." Jane felt sad attacking a helpless and outmoded god, but truth as she perceived it is truth. She had been enlightened by her magazine, her new, revised, up-to-date Bible. With a weak smile, Jane added thoughtfully, "If you should want to change your mind about things, I think I can get you into some feminist circles. Think about it."

Jane sighed heavily, giving Eden one last look. Curiously, she felt a tenderness to the God she was leaving. "Good-by, God. I've simply outgrown you."

Turning, Jane looked over the hill, beyond the boundary of Eden. Her face lit up. There she would find a city of flickering lights, liquor, and rock music; wild living to replace her peace. Office towers of Babel reached to the sky. Beginning on the ground floor, she could sleep and think her way to the top. "I can place my throne in the Starlight Room high above Eden," she thought. "I'm free of *No Trespassing* signs, of God interfering with my life, of narrow boundaries." Her face tingling, Jane raced to what cynical co-workers called a Sodom of sleaze, a Gomorrah of greed.

In Eden, Man awoke—and noticed the mirror. Puzzled, he picked it up. *Me, Jane*. What did it mean, he wondered. "Jane!" he called out. Noticing some of Jane's things were gone, he began to experience something strange. A word came to mind, and he called what he felt *worry*. That day he searched everywhere she might be. "J-A-N-E!"

By nightfall, the chill in the air and the darkness of the starless sky confirmed what he had come to realize: Jane had left him. He turned homeward. Jane's leaving was as painful as one of Man's ribs being ripped from his body, leaving his side bleeding. As painful as a wedding band of thorns pressed down on his head. Man was made to drink the bitter cup of Jane's rebellion.

I love Jane, thought Man. *And I'll stand by her through her wanderings. I'll pay the cost.* [11]

Jane applied for a job at *Trespass* Magazine. "Make it worth my while," leered the man in personnel, "and you've got the job." So Jane slept with him—and got the job. It wasn't so bad.

"Let's go away for the weekend," purred a woman higher-up, "and we'll talk about you becoming my assistant." Jane thought it a little strange at first, but by the second night of the weekend she was into the swing of it. Jane was learning in a hurry that "Lesbianism is the logical extension of feminism" and the true feminist will give lesbianism a serious try. [12]

"Cocaine gives you that aggressive edge," advised an older executive who was hearing footsteps gaining on him. "Try it. It'll keep you ahead of the pack." Jane tried it.

One day in the life of Jane began with an upper to get her started. Then to the clinic to see if her syphilis had cleared up. Next to the pharmacy for a dozen condoms and a morning-after pill, for when the condoms ran out. Next on the agenda was a stop at the de-tox center. Jane had made friends there during her stay to dry out. Next . . . Jane stopped for a moment. She was slowing down, yet there was so much to do. Catching her breath, Jane forced herself to speed up again.

If she hurried, she could work out at the spa. She used to get all the natural exercise she needed in Eden, but—well, why dredge up the past? After working out, she went to a Greek restaurant for a romantic lunch of gyros on pita bread. Slipping into the back room with her date, Jane used up another 20 minutes for an intimate affair. Cheating had become a way of life. Sure Man loved her, but now she was on the staff of a magazine and on the move with a full and exciting schedule! "I've become the woman I chose to be," boasted Jane.

Yet, Jane felt a power pulling her down. A heaviness seemed to follow her. "The answer," she thought, "is to outrun it." Moments of solitude brought only inner warfare, wrestling with the Beast. "Better to outrun the ancient dragon."

Flagging down a taxi, she went to a department store to buy a nonbaby gift for an abortion shower that weekend. Hopping into another cab, she stopped by a synagogue to transfer her tithe to Lesbians Forever! Her adrenaline racing, Jane took a cab to a government office where a woman can change her married name to her place of birth. "Jane Florida" had a nice, independent ring to it.

The hairstylist was next. Jane did want to look good for tonight, for she was scheduled to be the chapel speaker at a liberal, mainline School of Theology. Jane was mentally and physically tired. "Am I burned out? Is it worth it? Who out there even cares?! No," she thought, fighting off depression. "I can't give in. I've got to push on."[13]

Arriving at the School of Theology a little late, she was escorted to the platform. Following a flattering introduction by a woman professor on the staff, Jane rose and went to the pulpit. As she looked out from high up, faces blended into kingdoms of the world and then back into faces.[14] Jane spoke masterly:

"If God is a *Father* ruling *his* children . . . if God is in *his* heaven, then it is in the nature of things and by divine plan that men keep women under foot! This is what we learned at Daddy's knee—and from every Daddy ever since!"

"Yes."

"True."

"That's the way it is," responded voices from various places in the chapel.

"Well, I've got good news for you tonight. We don't have to give God human traits. God, you see, is a Verb!"

The students, caught off guard, didn't quite know how to respond, but they found the idea refreshing.

"There is an endless unfolding of God. God is a power of being which both is and is not yet. So participate in God the Verb and become your own woman in the process!"[15]

Smiling, the students applauded warmly.

"The new sisterhood I'm offering you is not 'brotherhood' but is revolution. The he-male, like Dracula, has lived on women's blood long enough, sapping energy from her until her death. What we want now is not 50/50, but restitution for stolen power and blood![16]

"We begin our journey on the boundaries of patriarchy's spaces and move out from there. Sisterhood is an exodus community moving from bondage toward liberation. Our covenant is not formed, but is an agreement among us that is found. The promise on which we march is in ourselves. The rhythm we hear as we march is communication, community and creation. The direction to which we march is not toward domination, but will eventually be egalitarian.

"There are no charts or maps for this journey into becoming androgynous beings, but we know the walls of *male* and *female* must come down, leaving only persons who are at one and the same time both male and female.[17] So as we all move out into new space, let us remember, 'The truth I am trying to grasp is the grasp that is trying to grasp it. . . . The Life I am trying to grasp is the me that is trying to grasp it.' "[18]

"Powerful!"

"Awesome!" called out the students, clapping loudly. "I don't know what it means, but did you hear it?"

"Fantastic . . ."

Jane smiled, appreciatively. "Some of you may not be interested in a If-It-Moves-Join-It religion. You may find it too abstract and cold. No fun. You may want the one who is developing to be a person, to be warm and have a history. For you, then, let me tell you of another world—one learned at *Mother's* knee."

Some chuckles were heard in the chapel.

"In the beginning, *Goddess* created the heavens and the earth, for all ancient peoples believed the world was created by a female deity. Her breasts and belly became symbols of birth and rebirth.[19] This Mother Goddess does not push away the male; She contains him, as a pregnant woman contains a male child. The Mother Goddess does not rule the world; She *is* the world.[20] And there is no male God outside of her looking down and frowning on what we do!"

Applause pleasantly interrupted Jane's talk. She resumed. "We believe in earliest times there was a Golden Age of Matriarchy,[21] and if there wasn't, it doesn't matter, for even inventing it puts pride and power into our present life.[22] By matriarchy, I don't mean simply that women ruled; I'm talking about a world-view where there are feelings of connectedness, of intuition, where power is not authoritarian and destructive.[23] But warlike men came to take away our power. We fought. Like Amazons we fought! *In every civilization we fought!* But we were beaten.[24] Men came to power. And today . . . *they still have the power!*"

"But not for long!" was the collective feeling of the female students.

"Today I tell you, we must throw out all the male gods and their baggage. If we don't, in times of bafflement people will crawl back.[25] In its place I offer you a better religion . . . the way of Witchcraft.[26] In witchcraft we replace God with the Goddess,[27] and in doing so, we affirm female power, the female body, the female will, and female heritage."[28]

Faces lit up in the chapel. Female students felt, "She's talking about *us!*"

"Witchcraft is a religion in which people revere women and draw power from the moon.[29] Our congregations are covens of some 13 people. There is no sin, because there are no commandments to sin against. Justice means to put a hex on those who wrong us. Because we do not live in a world of *good* and *evil,* our ethics are to love life and follow the life force. Our rituals are all acts of love and pleasure as the Goddess, who is within us, reveals herself. What we celebrate is worldly success and creativity. Because each woman is thought of as a Goddess, all of her creations are in a sense holy. What we celebrate is sex, for sex is sacred and to be celebrated."[30]

The men in the audience smiled and leaned forward. "Now we're getting somewhere."

"Yes," continued Jane, "there is a place for men in witchcraft. Their role is to make love to the Goddess and delight her. But never, never, never! do they rule. In witchcraft, the female rules the male! Always!"[31]

The females who were there with boyfriends looked playfully but sheepishly at their male companions. The guys didn't mind. "As long as I get what I want, who cares about all this mumbo jumbo."

Jane continued. "Our membership is this: You are a Witch by saying aloud, 'I am a Witch,' three times, and *thinking about that*. You are a Witch by being female, untamed, angry, joyous, and immortal.[32] So honor the Goddess in yourself. Put a mirror on the alter and worship her! For the Goddess whirls us in and out of existence. In the winking of her eye there is birth, death, and rebirth." Jane began crescendoing as she concluded, "I tell you tonight, each of us is her own star . . . her lover . . . *her Self!*"[33]

Applause broke out. Shouting out above the clapping, Jane called out, "I found God in myself . . ." Many in the audience rose to their feet and finished the litany: ". . . and I loved her fiercely."[34]

"I found God in myself," loudly intoned Jane.

". . . and I loved her fiercely!" responded the audience, even more students rising to their feet.

"*I found God in myself,*" loudly called out Jane.

". . . AND I LOVED HER FIERCELY!" cheered Jane and the audience together, everyone on their feet. To do your own female thing . . . what a joy it brought to female students and their liberal boyfriends.

Soon the organist was playing a sensual, Celtic melody. Many joined hands and, like one long serpent, began slithering through the chapel. Some young females went to the altar where there was a crucifix. Taking off their necklaces, which bore female images, they draped the necklaces on the cross. The young feminists, feeling the flush of liberation, then stripped off their clothes and danced naked before their female deity as they evolved a new ritual of love.[35]

One of the young females in the chapel was star-struck with Jane. She followed Jane like waxing follows the waning of the moon. Drained, Jane smiled weakly at the young woman. Yes, Jane would choose her. Taking the young female by the hand, Jane brought her home for the night.

Sex that night for Jane didn't feel either sacred or celebrated. Jane was just hoping to release some tension. How was it even possible to be filled with tension and feel empty at the same time!

Looking at the young female lying alongside her—what was her name?—Jane felt alone. Reaching for the bottle of sleeping pills on the nightstand, Jane took one. *"Trespass,"* thought Jane, still too keyed-up to sleep. *"Trespass* says I'm liberated. But for what? Why didn't the magazine tell me females are as jealous, possessive and domineering as the male? That a butch will not let her femme go to meetings where other women are present for fear of losing her to another lover? That one woman will love more and the other woman less? That a woman will walk out, abandoning her female lover without a word? That women can undress you with their eyes, looking at another woman as a sex object.[36] WHY?! Why did the magazine only feed me the make-believe side of life?" Shaking a few more sleeping pills into her cupped hand, Jane swallowed them.

Jane's thoughts floated back to Man and his colorful way of coming home: "OH-oh-OH-oh-OH-oh-O-O-O-O-O-O-H!" She smiled at the thought. "Love is so crazy, I actually miss him."[37] Becoming dreamy, she remembered how warm the water was in her pool. Wanting the peace that was lost, Jane took a few more sleeping pills.

The dreamlike water of Jane's vision now began swirling in slow-motion around her as though she were returning to the warmth of a womb. She reached over to touch Man—the bare shoulder beside her—as she had so often done in Eden. He loved her. In Eden, Jane had a sense of place, of purpose, of belonging. At last . . . Jane was being overcome by peace . . . Peace.

That night Jane died.

After the funeral, Man and Boy returned to Eden. It wasn't the same, of course. Standing on the edge of Eden—with it's sign restored—Man thought, "It all began with the magazine's little, trespassing voices. 'Be like me!' they encouraged. They were strange voices in Jane's life. From that day, the voice in the old missionary's Bible grew faint. 'My sheep hear my voice,' said the trusted old book. But Jane heard strange voices calling her to newer flocks: liquor, cocaine, lovers, strange causes, and a goddess."

Man looked over the home he called Eden. He felt peace, love. How different from the hurt and desolation east of Eden! What separated the two worlds? A wooden sign with the words burned in: *No Trespassing*.

Notes

1. Genesis 2:15 through chapter 3.
2. David Bouchier, *The Feminist Challenge,* Schocken Books, New York, 1984, p. 134.
3. Gabrielle Burton *I'm Running Away from Home But I'm Not Allowed to Cross the Street,* Know, Inc., Pittsburgh, 1972.
4. A companion essay to "Me, Jane" is "Who's the Boss?" on page 130.
5. **What the Bible says about God being spirit, not male**
   - God is a Spirit (a spiritual Being).
       —John 4:24 Amplified
   - For a spirit does not have flesh and bones . . .
       —Luke 24:39 Amplified
   - And Moses said to God, Behold, when I come to the Israelites and say to them, The God of your fathers has sent me to you, and they say to me, What is His name? What shall I say to them?

       And God said to Moses, I AM WHO I AM *and* WHAT I AM, *and* I WILL BE WHAT I WILL BE: and He said, You shall say this to the Israelites, I AM has sent me to you!
       —Exodus 3:13, 14 Amplified
   - Jesus said to them, Is not this where you wander out of the way and go wrong, because you know neither the Scriptures nor the power of God?

       For when they arise from among the dead, [men] do not marry nor are [women] given in marriage, but are like the angels in heaven.

       —Mark 12:24–25 Amplified
   - For as many of you as were baptized into Christ—into a spiritual union and communion with Christ, the Anointed One, the Messiah—have put on (clothed yourselves with) Christ. There is [now no distinction], neither Jew nor Greek, there is neither slave nor free, there is not male and female; for you are all one in Christ Jesus.
       —Galatians 3:27, 28 Amplified

Feminist literalism
Feminist fundamentalism is as primitive as . . . well . . . as the *mother goddess*. Rather than lower God to people's

earthly understanding, how liberating it would be to raise earthly understanding to know God as spirit, which is beyond male and female. The New Testament says:

> Infants in Christ. I gave you milk, not solid food, for you were not yet ready for it. Indeed, you are still not ready. You are still worldly. For since there is jealousy and quarreling among you, are you not worldly?
>
> —1 Corinthians 3:1–3 NIV

Meanwhile the earthbound quarreling goes on:

- God is male: Our *Father* which art in heaven
  > —Matthew 6:9 KJV, emphasis added.
- God/Christ is female: "How often would I have gathered your children together as a *mother* fowl gathers her brood under her wings."
  > —Matthew 23:37 Amplified, emphasis added.
- God has feathers: "He will cover you with his feathers, and under his wings. . ."
  > —Psalm 91:4 NIV
- Jesus is a door: "I am the Door."
  > —John 10:9 Amplified

What a gospel of clay to take into all the world! Would not the Lord say to quarrelers with this worldly point of view what he said to Peter:

> "Out of my way, Satan! . . . You stand right in my path, Peter, when you look at things from man's [a human] point of view and not from God's."
>
> —Matthew 16:23 Phillips

6. John 4:7–8.
7. Genesis 2:21–22.
8. Subjection is primarily a military term meaning to rank under (*Vine's Expository Dictionary*). The leader is not necessarily smarter or better than his followers. He simply is appointed as the source of direction to get on with winning the war.
   > —Miriam Neff in Andrea Hinding, *Feminism: Opposing Viewpoints*, Greenhaven Press, St. Paul, 1986, p. 136. See 2 Corinthians 6:14–7:1 and Ephesians 5:22.

9. Gloria Steinem, *Outrageous Acts and Everyday Rebellions*, Holt, Rinehart and Winston, New York, 1983, pp. 356–357.

10. Small, all-female, autonomous groups that meet to share personal experiences of sexism and analyze their common lot are doing "consciousness-raising" (CR). Among others: Bouchier, 86–88.

11. Ephesians 5:25.

12. Related in Ellen Peck, *a funny thing happened on the way to equality*, Prentice-Hall, Englewood Cliffs, NJ, 1975. pp. 134, 151.

13. **End of the feminist trail**
    What can a woman living the feminist life expect to find at the end of the trail? Gloria Steinem—a past and present feminist—confesses what her life of nearly 30 years in feminism was like.

    > Steinem, 57, says she now understands that her frantic life was less a positive choice than the destructive fallout from a lifetime of low self-esteem and ravenous self-doubt. . . .
    >
    > Whether she has considered the impact of this information on the legions of disillusioned 40-something superwoman isn't clear. . . .
    >
    > "Yet unlike other women with more self-vision, I believed so little in my own inner world that I couldn't stop to replenish it," she said. "Like a soldier who is wounded but won't lie down for fear of dying, I just kept marching."
    >
    > —Elinor Brecher, "Steinem's solo revolution: Discovering self-esteem changes famous feminist," Knight-Ridder News Service, *The San Diego Union*, January 22, 1992, pp. E-1, 3.

14. Matthew 4:8–10.

15. Mary Daly, *Beyond God the Father*, Beacon Press, Boston, 1973, pp. 13–43.

16. Daly, pp. 59, 172–173.

17. Daly, pp. 157–159.

18. R. D. Laing in Daly, p. 157.

19. Judy Chicago, "Our Heritage Is Our Power," in Charlene Spretnak (ed.), *The Politics of Women's Spirituality: Essays*

on the Rise of Spiritual Power within the Feminist Movement, Anchor Press, Doubleday & Co., Garden City, New York, 1982, pp. 152–153.

20. **What rule-by-women is like**
Rule-by-women is pictured as storybook beautiful, sensitive, and peaceful. A feminist in the 1970s, though, wrote this perceptive view:

> Fierce and somewhat mad squabbling has often broken out among feminists. Outrageous accusations of "revisionism" have been leveled; an unthinking insistence on lesbian supremacy has blossomed; as well as bitter character assassinations in the name of "elitism" and harsh pressure toward conformist opinion in the name of "sisterhood."
>
> —Vivian Gornick, *Essays in Feminism,* Harper & Row, New York, 1978, pp. 164–165.

22. Naomi Goldenberg, *Changing of the Gods: Feminism and the End of Traditional Religions,* Beacon Press, Boston, 1979, p. 89.

23. Margot Adler, "Meanings of Matriarchy," in Spretnak, p. 132.

24. Judy Chicago in Spretnak, p. 153.

25. Carol P. Christ, quoted by Starhawk in Spretnak, p. 51.

26. **What the Bible says about witchcraft**
From Moses, a prophet and lawgiver:

- When you enter the land the LORD your God is giving you, do not learn to imitate the detestable ways of the nations there. Let no one be found among you who sacrifices his son or daughter in the fire, who practices divination or sorcery, interprets omens, engages in witchcraft, or casts spells, or who is a medium or spiritist or who consults the dead. Anyone who does these things is detestable to the LORD, and because of these detestable practices the LORD your God will drive out those nations before you. You must be blameless before the LORD your God.

    The nations you will dispossess listen to those who practice sorcery or divination. But as for you, the LORD your God has not permitted you to do so. The LORD your God will raise up

for you a prophet like me from among your own brothers. You
must listen to him."
                              —Deuteronomy 18:9–15 NIV

• I am the Lord your god. You shall not eat anything with the
blood; neither shall you use magic, omens or witchcraft, [or
predict events by horoscope or signs and lucky days.].
                              —Leviticus 19:25, 26 Amplified

From the prophet Samuel:

To obey is better than sacrifice . . . For rebellion is as the sin
of witchcraft, and stubbornness is as idolatry and teraphim
(good luck images). Because you have rejected the word of the
Lord, He also has rejected you . . .
                              —1 Samuel 15:22, 23 Amplified

From the prophet Isaiah:

And when the people [instead of putting their trust in God]
shall say to you, Consult for direction mediums and wizards
who chirp and mutter, should not a people seek and consult
their God? Should they consult the dead on behalf of the living? [Direct such people] to the teaching and to the testi-
mony; if their teachings are not in accord with this word . . .
                              —Isaiah 8:19, 20 Amplified

From the New Testament church:

The name of the Lord Jesus was extolled and magnified. Many
also of those who were now believers came making full con-
fession and thoroughly exposing their [former deceptive and
evil] practices. And many of those who had practiced curious
magical arts collected their books and (throwing them book after book on the pile) burned them in the sight of everybody.
When they counted the value of them, they found it
amounted to fifty thousand pieces of silver (about $9,300).
Thus the Word of the Lord [concerning the attainment
through Christ of eternal salvation in the kingdom of God]
grew and spread and intensified, prevailing mightily.
                              —Acts 19:17–20 Amplified

27. What the Bible says about goddess worship and idolatry

•   "I am the LORD your God, who brought you out of Egypt,
out of the land of slavery.
"You shall have no other gods before me.

"You shall not make for yourself an idol in the form of anything in heaven above or on the earth beneath or in the waters below. You shall not bow down to them or worship them; for I, the LORD your God, am a jealous God, punishing the children for the sin of the fathers to the third and fourth generation of those who hate me, but showing love to thousands who love me and keep my commandments."

—Exodus 20:2–6 NIV

• Set your minds and keep them set on what is above—the higher things—not on the things that are on the earth. For [as far as this world is concerned] you have died, and your [new, real] life is hid with Christ in God. When Christ Who is our life appears, then you also will appear with Him in (the splendor of His) glory.

So kill (deaden, deprive of power) the evil desire lurking in your members—those animal impulses and all that is earthly in you that is employed in sin: sexual vice, impurity, sensual appetites, unholy desires, and all greed and covetousness, for that is idolatry [the deifying of self and other created things instead of God].

—Colossians 3:2–5 Amplified

28. Carol P. Christ, "Why Women Need the Goddess," in Spretnak, p. 74.
29. Anne Kent Rush, "The Politics of Feminist Spirituality," in Spretnak, p. 383.
30. Starhawk, "Witchcraft," and "Ethics and Justice in Goddess Religion," in Spretnak, pp. 53, 419. Plus, Goldenberg, pp. 93, 102, 112–113.
31. Goldenberg, pp. 103–104.
32. "New York Covens" in Robin Morgan (ed.), *Sisterhood is Powerful: Anthology of Writings from the Women's Liberation Movement*, Random House, New York, 1970, p. 540.
33. Starhawk, "Witchcraft," in Spretnak, pp. 55–56.
34. Ntozake Shange in her stageplay *for colored girls who have considered suicide/when the rainbow is enuf* quoted in Christ, "Why Women Need the Goddess," in Spretnak, p. 71.

35. See Goldenberg, pp. 92–93.

36. **The myth of being a Christian feminist**

Jesus cannot be stuffed into the feminist bag, along with
>   Mother goddesses
>   Lesbian lovers
>   "I-have-chosen-me" preacher-women
>   Two-headed homes
>   Women aping sinful men
>   Abortions in a jiffy.

Consider instead a Lord who is above gunny sacks:

- But seek for (aim at and strive after) first of all His kingdom, and His righteousness [His way of doing and being right] . . .
  >   —Matthew 6:33 Amplified
- No one can serve two masters . . .
  >   —Matthew 6:24 Amplified
- In his own account of his conversion, the church father, Jerome, who made the Latin translation of the Bible, tells of a dream that led to his conversion. He dreamed, he says, that he appeared before the Judge. Asked who and what he was, he replied, "I am a Christian." But he who presided said: "Thou liest, thou art a follower of Cicero, not of Christ." For Jerome was a rhetorician and his consuming interest and first love was his study of Cicero.
  >   —Frank E. Gaebelein, *The Christian, The Arts, And Truth,* Multnomah, Portland, Oregon, 1985, p. 172. A rhetorician (ret′ oh RISH an) is an eloquent writer or speaker.
- Elijah then came near to all the people, and said, "How long will you go limping with two different opinions? If the LORD is God, follow him; but if Baal, then follow him." The people did not answer him a word.
  >   —1 Kings 18:21 New RSV

36. Peck, pp. 139, 150–154.

37. "Your desire and craving shall be for your husband."
>   —Genesis 3:16 Amplified

"Heaven is my throne,
  and the earth is my footstool."
        —Isaiah 66:1 NIV

Who's the Boss?

IN THE HOME

When a Couple "Lives Together," Guess Who's Boss?

WHO'S the boss when lovers are "in a relationship" and are living together?

It was Friday evening. Ever hopeful, Chrissy hurried to the Happy Hour. It was while sipping a margarita that her eyes fell upon Troy. He returned her look. Chrissy was so surprised when after a few moments he came toward her, she began choking on the corn chips she was nibbling.

"Is there room for me in your life?" he asked smoothly. Hours passed. As laughter went up and margaritas went down, Chrissy's neon lit up within her. "He's the one!" it flashed. She looked at Troy and imagined running hand in hand with him through their wedding rice.

He touched her knee. Chrissy's heart pounded to the big beat of the band's "Boom. Boom-boom. Boom. Boom-boom." As the evening soared, the magic happened—Troy asked, "Your place or mine?"

Chrissy didn't hear the words because the band's "Boom. Boom-boom" hit 110 decibels, but she had long ago learned to read lips—at least phrases like "Would you like to go outside for a while?" and "Is there a more quiet place we can go to get to know each other?" To Troy's invitation, Chrissy flushed and answered, "My apartment."

It didn't take Troy and Chrissy long to go from the door to the sofa, where passions rose and inhibitions dropped. Troy whispered, "Let's practice making babies." Chrissy wanted to say, "I'm saving that for my husband," but she felt embarrassed. *Too old-fashioned,* she thought. So she said nothing—and followed the "Boom. Boom-boom" of her body to the bedroom.

The next morning Chrissy awoke after Troy had left. Dreamily putting on a robe, she went to the kitchen. There on the refrigerator door was a note. It was held in place by a kitchen magnet shaped like a tilted cocktail glass. It read:

MEMO
What a bod!
See ya tonight
—T

"Oooo," squealed Chrissy. Yes, it was lust at first sight for both of them.

A week later Troy and Chrissy had a housewarming party to celebrate their living together. It was at the party that Troy asked Chrissy to be monogamous, to see only him. "Of course," she purred faithfully. After all, hadn't they consummated being "in a relationship" the first night? While Chrissy felt bonded to her man, Troy explained, "I'm not ready yet to see you exclusively. That's a big commitment for me. I need time." Chrissy understood.

As days passed and lifestyle evolved, their who-does-what drifted into the usual arrangement for couples living together.

THE LIBERATED MAN	THE LIBERATED WOMAN
Pays ½ the rent	Pays ½ the rent
	Shops for food
	Cooks the food
	Washes food off the dishes
	. . . and gives her lover sex.
	Dusts the furniture & ceiling
	Vacuums carpets & drapes
	Scrubs the bathtub & sinks
	. . . and gives her lover sex.
	Picks up socks & underwear
	Washes socks & underwear
	Puts away socks & underwear
Changes light bulbs.	. . . and gives her lover sex.

One morning Chrissy saw a note on the refrigerator door. The note was held in place by the magnet of the tilted cocktail glass. It read simply:

MEMO
Good-by.
—T

Chrissy's "Boom. Boom-boom" came to a sudden stop. "He even added a period," she bawled, "to *Good-by*."

A month of Fridays passed. Then another month. Picking up her tired bones, her debased spirit, her worries about one day hitting 30, Chrissy trudged to the hottest happy hour in town—there to begin another round.

Troy and Chrissy were a twosome, but at every turn, at every testing, they invited Satan along. At the bar, it was Satan who kept the margaritas coming. When Troy asked "Your place or mine?" it was Satan who played the "Boom. Boom-boom" on the drum of Chrissy's heart. It was Satan who later whispered, "Don't be old-fashioned." When the housewarming party was scheduled, Satan mailed out the invitations.

Satan felt comfortable in the twosome's let's-play-house-of-a-home. He's pleased with homes that are spiritually vacant. When Troy and Chrissy watched TV, Satan turned the channels. When the twosome ate, there was a third person at the table passing the fruit of his spirit: suspicion, jealousy, quarreling, and exploitation. When the twosome went to bed, it was a threesome, a ménage à trois of man, woman, and lustful Satan. When Troy wrote the MEMO *Good-by.*—it was Satan who added the period.

Who's the boss? In a living together relationship, Satan smiles knowingly.

In a Christian home, who's the boss? It's not the husband, the wife, the teen-ager, or the "terrible two." Who but Christ, whose presence fills every room. In the living room, Christ is the living Word.

> Whatsoever things are true, whatsoever things are honest, whatsoever things are just, whatsoever things are pure, whatsoever things are lovely, whatsoever things are of good report; if there be any virtue, and if there be any praise, think on these things.[1]

In the closet of the home, the Spirit hovers:

> For the LORD searches every heart and understands every motive behind the thoughts.[2]

In the bedroom, the Holy Spirit, who helped to fashion man and woman naked and unashamed, unites two flesh into one. In the kitchen, the Creator feeds the family

> . . . foods which God created to be received with thanksgiving . . . For everything God has created is good, and nothing is to be thrown away or refused if it is received with thanksgiving. For it is hallowed and consecrated by the Word of God and by prayer.[3]

On the refrigerator door—held in place by a magnet shaped like a strawberry—is a reminder:

MEMO
Christ rules the husband[4]
The husband-in-Christ rules the wife[5]
The wife (parents) rules the child[6]
The child rules the cocker spaniel
The cocker spaniel rules the back yard.

Couples who keep their head in order will have a peace that passes understanding in their homes.

IN THE CHURCH

Does God Call Women To Teach, Preach and Oversee?

Does God call women to preach? In modern times, Kathryn Kuhlman preached the Word, with signs of healings and salvation following.[7] Does God call women to teach men, and to teach with authority? In the New Testament, Priscilla more fully taught Apollos.[8]

Does God call women to make top-level decisions in the church? In the Old Testament, Deborah was a prophet(ess) and a Judge. She sat under a tree giving divinely-inspired judgments as both men and women came to her for decisions.[9] Does God call women to pray and prophesy in public worship and does he want them to show forth the nine miraculous gifts of the spirit?[10] Yes!

Now here's a little quiz. What words leaped from the page in reading the above?

( ) *Kathryn? Priscilla? Deborah?* All women, of course.
( ) *With authority . . . taught Apollos . . . top-level.* All words about power.
( ) *Signsofhealings . . . salvationfollowing . . . divinely-inspired . . . miraculous gifts of the spirit.* All spirit-

ual words. To have these words light up your soul takes the eyes and heart of a servant.

This may seem like an innocent pop quiz, but it underlies the whole matter of who's the head, the boss, the ruler of the church. The answer in Scripture is plain enough. Who's boss? Well, it's not the male, female, pope, bishop, cardinal, pastor, president, elder, or deacon. The answer is "Christ."

Christ is the head of the church, his body[11]

The head of the spiritual, invisible church is Christ. The head of the earthly, local, day-to-day church is Christ. "MY church," said Jesus.[12]

There is a power play in the earthly church between men and women. In the "absence" of Jesus on earth, each side comes armed with Scriptures. But all the Scriptures point to Jesus Christ as head of the visible church.

Let's look at some of the troublesome Scriptures, the ones that seem to leap out for one side or the other.

In Christ there is neither male nor female[13]

A wonderful fact. But it doesn't say which person Christ Jesus calls to be bishop, shepherd, teacher . . . or janitor.

Wh♀s♀ever will may c♀me

A phrase based on "Whosoever shall call on the name of the Lord shall be saved."[14] But salvation isn't the same as leadership. Jesus said, "You did not choose me, but I chose you"[15]— as earthly disciples, preachers, followers, servants. Nothing has changed.[16]

Women should remain silent in the churches[17]

Why? Because chattering during worship is chaotic and worship is meant to be orderly. In context, Paul is talking about worship being orderly. (Yes, ladies, this would also refer to chattering men, but that was not the problem at hand.)

I do not permit a woman to teach or to have authority over a man; she must be silent.[18]
Based on the Bible as a whole, we might interpret Paul to mean: Personally, I do not permit a woman, simply because she wants to be equal to men or whose only credential is her sex, to have authority over a man. In the church body—based on sex alone—a woman (or a man) must be silent.

In light of the complete Bible, we might understand Paul, who is answering feminists, to mean: A woman may teach and oversee only if she is called and anointed as a servant by the head of the church, who alone is Christ.

How do we know a woman-leader (or male-leader) is called, empowered, and given authority by Christ? By looking at her
• spiritual fruit
• spiritual gifts
• and signs following.[19]
Signs are earthly fruit. They are people being saved,[20] healings happening, words of knowledge being spoken, and various gifts of the spirit illumining like a light turned on! The signs may be seen in the shepherdess or her flock. Signs are meant to be everyday happenings in a church where the living Lord is head.

Remember the little quiz at the start? A woman who saw only the power words might forget that the role of pastoring and overseeing in the church is not a career—it's a calling.

Adam was formed first, then Eve[21]
Yet in the Bible a person's first birth is earthly while his/her second birth is spiritual, so the older may serve the younger. The older Esau served the younger Jacob. And remember how the older brothers of Joseph bowed like sheaves of grain before their younger brother?[22]

It was Eve and not Adam who was first deceived?[23]
At the time of her fall, Eve's order of "who's the boss?" was from top to bottom: Eve-husband-God. It didn't work, and that's why she was deceived first. Eves need to be under the headship of a godly husband in the home and under the headship of Christ in the church: God-husband-Eve.

The head of the woman is[24]
(   ) **man,** a sex
(✔) **her husband,** a relationship freely chosen.
In context, *husband* is the better translation. (The same Greek word means *man* or *husband*.) This is not a Scripture giving males rule over females in churches, on the job, on the street, in school, at parties, or on dates.

He shall rule over you
The fuller Scripture reads: "Your *husband,* and he shall rule over you."[25] No male dominance here, either. In the home, the husband is to love and sacrifice for his bride as Christ did for the church.[26]

While the battle of the sexes continues into the church, the matter was settled long ago about who rules. "MY church," said Jesus simply.[27] Maybe we should return the church to her rightful owner . . .

IN THE WORLD

Who's the boss? From the highest star to the lowest shellfish, there is a divine order in our universe. Were the sky a writing pad, in giant letters could be written:

MEMO
God rules the world[28]
Christ rules the church[29]
Government rules the citizen[30]
(Godly) Husband rules the wife[31]
Parent rules the child[32]
People rule creatures[33]
Sun rules the day[34]
Moon rules the night.[35]

So from star to shellfish, that's who is boss!

Notes

1. Philippians 4:8 KJV.
2. 1 Chronicles 28:9 NIV.
3. 1 Timothy 4:3–5 Amplified.
4. The head of every man is Christ . . .
   > —1 Corinthians 11:3 NIV
5. **The Husband-in-Christ**
   - Christ is the head of every man, the head of a woman is her husband.
     > —1 Corinthians 11:3 Amplified. "Husband" also in the New RSV and Smith-Goodspeed. See the footnotes on 11:3 in the NIV Study Bible and in the New RSV.
   - "Your husband, and he will rule over you."
     > —Genesis 3:16 NIV
   - Wives, submit to your husbands as to the Lord. For the husband is the head of the wife as Christ is the head of the church, his body, of which he is the Savior. Christ loved the church . . . cleansing her . . . to present her . . . radiant . . . without stain . . . holy . . . In this same way, husbands ought to love their wives . . .
     > —Ephesians 5:22–28 NIV

   The Husband-outside-of-Christ
   If Bonnie marries Clyde, she doesn't have to rob banks because hubby tells her to. Christ-in-Scripture still rules:
   - You shall not steal.
     > —Ten Commandments. Exodus 20:15 New RSV.
   - "We must obey God rather than any human authority."
     > —Acts 5:29 New RSV
6. • "Honor your father and mother"
     > —Exodus 20:12 NIV
   - Children, obey your parents in the Lord
     > —Ephesians 6:1 NIV
7. My purpose is to save souls, and my particular calling is to offer proof of the Power of God. . . .

   If you believe that I, as an individual, have any power to heal, you are dead wrong. . . . I have no healing power whatsoever. All I can do is point you to the Way—I can lead you to the Great Physician and I can pray; but the rest is left with you and God. . . .

All healing is Divine, whether it is physical or spiritual; but of the two . . . spiritual healing is the greater.

> —Kathryn Kuhlman, *I Believe in Miracles*, Pyramid Books, New York, 1972, pp. 11, 15–16, 19.

8. Acts 18:24–26.

9. Judges 4:4–9.

10. **Women in public may pray, prophesy, and show forth gifts**

And any woman who [publicly] prays or prophesies (teaches, refutes, reproves, admonishes or comforts) . . .

> —1 Corinthians 11:5 Amplified

Now I wish that you might *all* speak in [unknown] tongues . . .

> —1 Corinthians 14:5 Amplified, emphasis added.

This is [the beginning of] what was spoken through the prophet Joel:

And it shall come to pass in the last days, God declares, that I will pour out of My Spirit upon *all* mankind, and your sons and your *daughters* shall prophesy—telling forth the divine counsels . . .

> —Acts 2:16, 17 Amplified, emphasis added.

11. Ephesians 5:23 NIV. See Ephesians 1:22 and Colossians 1:18.

12. Matthew 16:18, emphasis added.

13. There is neither Jew nor Greek, slave nor free, male nor female, for you are all one in Christ Jesus.

> —Galatians 3:28 NIV

14. Acts 2:21 KJV.

15. **Jesus Christ chooses church leaders**

You did not choose me, but I chose you and appointed you to go and bear fruit—fruit that will last.

> —John 15:16 NIV

So *God* has appointed some in the church (for His own use): first apostles (special messengers); second prophets (inspired preachers and expounders); third teachers, then wonder-workers, then those with ability to heal the sick, helpers, administrators, [speakers in] different [unknown] tongues.

—1 Corinthians 12:28 Amplified, emphasis added. See Exodus 31:1–11.

16. Jesus Christ is the same yesterday and today and forever.

—Hebrews 13:8 NIV

17. 1 Corinthians 14:34 NIV.

- For God is not a God of disorder but of peace.

—1 Corinthians 14:33 NIV

- But all things should be done with regard to decency and propriety and in an orderly fashion.

—1 Corinthians 14:40 Amplified

18. 1 Timothy 2:12 NIV.

19. **How to know a leader is called by Christ**

- By their fruit you will recognize them.

—Matthew 7:16 NIV

- The *fruit of the Spirit* is love, joy, peace, patience, kindness, goodness, faithfulness, gentleness and self-control.

—Galatians 5:22 NIV, emphasis added.

The nine *gifts of the spirit* given for the common good are a word of wisdom, a word of knowledge, faith, gifts of healings, working of miracles, prophecy, discerning true from false spirits, speaking unknown tongues (languages), and interpreting these tongues. (1 Corinthians 12:7–10)

- "You must go out to the whole world and proclaim the Gospel to every creature. . . . These signs will follow those who do believe: they will drive out evil spirits in my name; they will speak with new tongues; they will pick up snakes, and if they drink anything poisonous it will do them no harm; they will lay their hands upon the sick and they will recover."

After these words to them, the Lord Jesus was taken up into Heaven and was enthroned at the right hand of God. They went out and preached everywhere. *The Lord worked with them, confirming* their message *by the signs that followed.*

—Mark 16:15, 17–20 Phillips, emphasis added.

20. And the Lord was adding to their number day by day those who were being saved.

—Acts 2:47 NAS

21. 1 Timothy 2:13 NIV
22. **The older serving the younger**
    The first man (was) from out of earth, made of dust—earth-minded; the second Man (is) *the Lord* from out of heaven. (Gen. 2:7) Now those who are made of the dust are like him who was first made of the dust—earth-minded; and as is (the Man) from heaven, so also (are those) who are of heaven—heaven-minded.
    > —1 Corinthians 15:47–48 Amplified. See also, John 3:1–7.

    She was told, "The older will serve the younger." Just as it is written: "Jacob I loved, but Esau I hated." . . . It is not the natural children who are God's children, but it is the children of the promise who are regarded as Abraham's offspring.
    > —Romans 9:12–13, 8, NIV

    Joseph had a dream, and when he told it to his brothers, they hated him all the more. He said to them, "Listen to this dream I had: We were binding sheaves of grain out in the field when suddenly my sheaf rose and stood upright, while your sheaves gathered around mine and bowed down to it."
    > —Genesis 37:5–7 NIV
23. 1 Timothy 2:14 Phillips.
24. 1 Corinthians 11:3. *Man* in the KJV, NAS, and NIV translations. *Husband* in the Amplified, New RSV and Smith-Goodspeed translations. See the footnotes on 11:3 in the NIV Study Bible and in the New RSV.
25. Genesis 3:16 Amplified, New RSV, New KJV, NAS, emphasis added. *Husband* also in NIV, KJV, and Smith-Goodspeed.
26. Ephesians 5:22–28. See note 5 in these Notes.
27. Matthew 16:18, emphasis added.
28. "Heaven is my throne, and the earth is my footstool."
    > —Isaiah 66:1 NIV
29. Ephesians 5:23 and 1:22. Colossians 1:18. Matthew 16:18.
30. Let every person be loyally subject to the governing (civil) authorities. For there is no authority except from God—by his permission, His sanction; and those that exist do so by God's appointment. (Prov. 8:15)

Therefore he who resists and sets himself up against the authorities resists what God has appointed and arranged—in divine order.

—Romans 13:1–2 Amplified.
See 1 Peter 2:13–17.

31. Genesis 3:16. Ephesians 5:22–23. 1 Corinthians 11:3 Amplified, New RSV, and Smith-Goodspeed.

32. Exodus 20:12. Ephesians 6:1.

33. Fill the earth and subdue it (with all its vast resources); and have dominion over the fish of the sea, the birds of the air, and over every living creature that moves upon the earth.

—Genesis 1:28 Amplified

34. And God made the two great lights, the greater light (the sun) to rule the day . . .

—Genesis 1:28 Amplified

35. . . . and the lesser light (the moon) to rule the night.

—Genesis 1:16 Amplified

For he himself is our peace,
who has made the two one
and has destroyed the barrier,
the dividing wall of hostility.
—Ephesians 2:14 NIV

Civil War

THE Civil War was fought in the 1860s. Or was it the 1960s?

The Battle of Montgomery was a stunning victory for the rebs. Moving swiftly, they claimed victory by proving an army moves on its feet.

The spark touching off the war was set by Rosa Parks, returning home from her civilian job as a seamstress. Tired after working all day, she sat in the back of the bus, in the first row of the colored section. The white bus driver called back, "You Negroes in the first row get up so white folks can sit down."[1] Those were fightin' words!

Parks fired back, "Why should I give up my seat to a white man? I paid the same fare he did." Arrested and jailed, Parks was fined $10. Was this incident to be the rallying hour for the rebs? Colonel E. D. Nixon, leader of the Montgomery Rebs, would decide.

Earlier that year a fifteen-year-old girl was similarly arrested on a bus. Reb Colonel Nixon passed on her when it was learned she had "taken a tumble"—was pregnant. She might look to whites as a "bad girl" just making trouble. But looking at Rosa Parks, the Colonel knew her to be a proven soldier serving an enlistment in the NAACP. He decided. "War is declared!"

E. D. Nixon was an outspoken, cussin' Pullman-car porter who had a sixth grade education. He was a fightin' general, not one to wait for the courtroom to take maybe a century to bring rebs their freedom. His military strategy was simple:

> We'd talked about the bus boycott all year. I kept saying the only way we're going to do any good is to hit these people right where it hurts, and that's in the pocketbook. We goin' to have to boycott these buses.[2]

A rally was called. A young reb lieutenant Martin Luther King Jr. was present. He would soon rise up the ranks. As the rebels rallied 'round the flag, they hollered, "Don't ride the bus on Monday!" Little did anyone know the one-day battle would become a 13-month seige.

Until demands for respect were granted, 40,000 rebels would not put their coins in the collection boxes on buses each day. Rather, they would walk or ride in cabs driven by reb drivers, who would only charge a dime. The whites counterattacked. Union General Sellers, a hard-liner, made it known these drivers would be heavily fined if they did not charge the minimum forty-five-cent fare.

The rebs, now under the command of General King, created a complex plan of carpooling with drop-off and pick-up points. Nixon, a modest man, wanted to turn the troops over to King, a man he felt was better educated, new in the community, and who had a strong moral image as a reverend.

Union Sergeant Crenshaw formulated the strategy for the whites:

> If we granted the Negroes these demands, they would go about boasting of a victory that they had won over the white people, and this we will not stand for.[3]

With many rebs getting up at 3:00 a.m. to walk to work, the bus company and downtown businesses were losing money, not white or black money—green money. With quiet dignity, the rebels marched to work—no mass battles, no nasty confrontations—just each reb going to his own place of work. On they marched, through winter, spring, into the summer of '56.

The whites, meanwhile, entrenched. Union General Gayle asked housewives not to drive their maids to work. But wives of soldiers wondered, "Is Gayle gonna wash the dirty dishes, hang out the wet clothes, and change dirty diapers for us?" Housework shortages were being felt as the home front fell into disarray.

The decisive battle—fought in a courthouse—came in the winter of '56 when the Supreme Court outlawed segregation on Alabama buses. The Battle of Montgomery was over. Some diehards became snipers or bombed homes and churches, but the battle was a brilliant victory for the rebs. General King wrote in his notes that the Battle of Montgomery was the story of 50,000 foot soldiers

> who were willing to substitute tired feed for tired souls and walk the streets of Montgomery until the walls of segregation were finally battered by the forces of justice![4]

King preached, "We must meet hate with love." He believed, "As we go back to the buses, let us be loving enough to turn an enemy into a friend." The problem King would agonize over and never fully resolve was

> How could I make a speech that would be militant enough to keep my people aroused to positive action and yet moderate enough to keep this fervor within controllable Christian bounds?[5]

Sadly for the nation, King's strategy in Montgomery of walk-to-work-minding-your-own-business would evolve into a militant warfare of hit-'em-with-peace and sock-'em-with-nonviolence. Evolving through mass marches and eyeball-to-eyeball confrontations, King would end

> . . . seeking tactics which would be still more dynamic, and he spoke of massive "dislocation" of transportation systems, of local bureaucracies, perhaps of the government itself.[6]

Poking, provoking, and attacking simply did not bring love to the hearts of his victims. Meanwhile, the civil war continued.

The Lunch Counter Campaign of '60 was a series of skirmishes by, among others, the Greensboro Boys and Lawson's Raiders. Rebel students simply walked into a five and dime and sat quietly at the segregated lunch counter, waiting to be served. In '60, privately-owned businesses could serve whom they wished—a type of "no shoes, no shirt, no service" approach. The sit-in was a classic conflict of privately owned vs. privately desired. Yet something was happening that was "bigger than a hamburger."[7]

A few Northern whites felt as former Union President Truman did:

> If anyone came into my store and tried to stop business, I'd throw him out.[8]

Most Northern whites, however, felt the sit-in skirmishes were romantic, quaint, and far away—where someone else eats lunch. Further, they were nonthreatening, for who marries the guy sitting next to you at a 5 & 10?

Some TV war correspondents—who seemingly checked in their ethics for a camera—learned to stage events for the media. With tongue-in-cheek they could truthfully tell their sit-down viewers, "You are seeing *history in the making*."

Whites who lived where the forays were happening found sit-ins left a bad taste. Sometimes the response was heckling: "How about a date when we integrate?" Sometimes it was pouring ketchup over a reb's head. Neither side could imagine the warfare that lay ahead, a time when the ketchup would turn to blood.

In the Wilderness Campaign of the early '60s, a scattering of gunshots was heard as rebs signed up people to vote. It's easy to vote in America—unless you live in the wilderness where hobgoblins of white hate and boogeymen of black fears and white fears go bump in the night. It took guts to fight in the wilderness, and young rebs penetrated the gloom with courage.

Rebel General King and his lieutenants were smarting from a defeat in Albany, Georgia. Taking his nonviolence to the streets had resulted in his troops throwing rocks. Said foxy Union Colonel Pritchett, who outmaneuvered King, "Did you see them nonviolent rocks?"[9] To avoid further defeats, King felt better strategy was needed.

Meeting with his lieutenants, King carefully laid plans for the Battle of Birmingham. They called the plan Project "C"—for "Confrontation." The goal: desegregate Birmingham's downtown businesses. The date: March of '63, the holy season.

Whites meanwhile had ousted Birmingham's "Bull Dog" Connor, a ferocious Union general. But King's attack would occur during the changing of the guard, a time when both Bull Dog and a moderate new leader would be in charge. Some downtown merchants the year before had taken down their *Colored Only* signs from lunch counters, restrooms, and drinking fountains. "Put 'em back up!" barked the Bull Dog of the Union, waving papers of building-code violations.

White merchants and clergy were upset with General King's rebel plan for confrontation. As a spokesman said of King, "He wouldn't give us a chance to prove what we could do through the political processes."[10] A court order forbidding King and other known reb soldiers to march, organize, or confront was issued. But Project "C" called for King to be arrested on Good Friday. If the court order were obeyed, the script couldn't be followed and the TV cameras would go dark. What would "de Lawd" do? "De Lawd" is how young, militant, SNCCering[11] rebs referred to King because he got all the front page coverage. Well, de Lawd marched, was arrested, and was jailed. To the chapter and verse, his Project "C" was working!

From the Birmingham jail, General King ruminated about questions asked of him by clergymen:

> Why direct action? Why sit-ins, marches, and so forth? Isn't negotiation a better path?[12]

Writing in the margins of a newspaper and on scraps of toilet paper, King replied

> There comes a time when the cup of endurance runs over, and men are no longer willing to be plunged into the abyss of despair. I hope, sirs, you can understand our legitimate and unavoidable impatience . . . [13]

Love may be patient and kind,[14] but warfare gets results. Found guilty of civil contempt, King was released pending appeal.[15]

Back at the motel, King and his lieutenants planned the next phase of Project "C." The idea: a children's crusade! Gathering 1,000 children and telling them he was proud of them, General King sent them into battle. The children, in age six to eighteen, marched into "Bull Dog" Connor's savage dogs and into powerful streams of water from firefighters. The water catapulted the children against curbs, over parked cars, and rolled them down streets. Several youngsters were attacked by dogs. Project "C" was a masterpiece of scripting Birmingham into "Bombingham." The TV cameras rolled!

TV war correspondents gleefully covered the dog-bites-man episodes, missing the deeper story of reb-bites-dog. As families across America sat by their fireplaces in shock, the evening news eagerly fed the firewood, fanning the flames of war.

Fearing greater violence, white merchants hastily agreed to desegregate lunch counters and to hire black workers. The response from whites: bombs, clubs and rifles. From rebs: rampaging, looting, and setting fire to seven stores. The Union president, Kennedy, ordered troops to Fort McClellan, on the outskirts of Birmingham. The cup of everyone's endurance was running over. Finally, the moderate mayor who had been elected took over, bringing the Battle of Birmingham to an end.

How much "love" King left in the hearts of his Birmingham foes is hard to say because of the police dogs, fire hoses, clubs, and bombs. Certainly his I-Love-You-Birmingham would be forever burned into their hearts.

The war had its Western theater—California, where palm trees grow. If you were to find a coconut palm growing in the ghetto of Watts, clustered among its arching fronds would be the hard coconuts of absent fathers, feelings of inferiority, teenage pregnancies, prostitution, dropouts and illiteracy, unemployment, anger, gangs, addictions, crime, unfulfilled expectations, police harassment, and uprootedness. If someone should ever shake such a tree, the coconuts would fall with many "bangs" and conk many heads. The coconuts fell on August 11 of '65.

A squad on patrol gave a reb a traffic ticket, and things got out of hand. A crowd of rebels gathered. What would they do? What they had seen on TV—take to the streets!

"This is just like Birmingham," hollered one reb.

"Get Whitey," shouted rebs, running down streets.

"Burn, baby, burn!" cried another, taking a harmless phrase of the day and putting it to hell-fire use.[16] Ten- to thirty- and upwards to eighty thousand exhilarated rebs would soon be singing, "There's gonna be a hot time in the old town tonight!" After looting white businesses of guns, cameras, liquor, TV sets, and mattresses, the stores were set ablaze.

Strange sights were seen: looters stopping at traffic lights waiting for the signal to change, while carrying home in one hand stolen goods and in the other hand violence, "as American as cherry pie."[17] A couple carrying a heavy sofa would, from time to time, set the sofa down and rest on it.[18] Scrawling the words "Soul Brother" on a window saved many stores owned by rebs.

Orange flames swallowed up rooftops. Black plumes of Death rose into the smoky air. Looters in a Dante-esque dance reveled in the nightmare.

Union General William Parker called for a counterattack. Nearly 14,000 Guardsmen with armored divisions of jeeps -with-machine-guns cleared streets. They reinforced LAPD units, who were searching out urban guerrillas. Sirens screamed, civilians yelled, guns fired, Molotov cocktails were thrown, flames leaped, smoke billowed. The toll: 34 dead. Said a Union general, "War is hell."[19]

With shouts of "Reb Power!" the rebels expanded and escalated the war with their March through the North. While "tenting tonight," these troops would read Malcolm X, Mao, and Che Guevera. The Old Guard shook their heads, "God help black Americans if this is their revolution and these their revolutionaries."[20]

Using a "scorched earth" policy, this time it was the rebs who made a March to the Sea, laying seige to cities from Los Angeles to Detroit to Washington during '65 to '68. Americans watched in horror as their cities blazed red with fire and ran red with blood. As people stared, the pipe dream of "confrontation is nonviolent" burned to ash before their eyes. Sickened by the madness, both sides eventually trudged back to their homes, their energy spent, their feet as tired as Rosa Parks.

When rebs marched, walls came tumbling down. But who would rebuild? The rebs went home holding a piece of paper, "Equal Rights." Yet a generation later, cold hearts, poverty, unemployment, ghettos, and tension between whites and rebs remained. The paper is the letter of the law. But what of the spirit? Who can fulfill the law of the earth?

Liberation movements are of the earthly spirit, taking a little from God's spirit, taking a little from Satan's, taking whatever serves the human spirit, mainly earthly "things": voting rights, better jobs, more pay, and homes on the right side of the tracks. But this earthly spirit is met by an opposing earthly spirit, which offers no voting, poorer jobs, less pay, and homes on the "other side" of the tracks. Meanwhile, as the two sides march, they dig their heels into the face of love.

At the foot of the Cross the war will be won. When blacks and whites march there in surrender, peace will prevail. Black marchers will have to leave at the foot of the cross all their weapons and attitudes of war:

low self-esteem, as though God did not create blackness

anxiety about what to eat, drink, and wear

sense of injustice, of being discriminated against in an unfair world

resentments, bitterness

with a 6,000 year heritage of freedom, dwelling on slave days: "I ain't nothing today because of what you did to my great-great-granddaddy down South 150 years ago. Remember?"

blaming the "Man," the "Boss," the blue-eyed white devil for black problems[21]

coveting white neighbors' schools, homes, and jobs

demands for jobs and college admissions based on color not merit

demands for memorials, honors and earthly praise:
of streets named for generals
of birthdays for fallen soldiers, birthdays forced to be observed[22]

lust for power

anger

provoking to anger

rebellion

wildness: gangs, crime, burning, looting, drugs, promiscuity, profanity

unbelief in God working things out

impatience with whites and with God.

Whites will have to come to the Cross and drop their weapons and attitudes of war:

white superiority
racial fear and hate, a white minority in a colored, global village
keeping minorities under the thumb
tiredness and resentment in paying welfare to a colored underclass
fear of minorities proving themselves to be "as much a man"
insecurity in a nuclear world
frustration on the job
fear whites can no longer make it, in the eyes of whites and in the eyes of others
running from responsibility and personal commitment
greed, a lust for things
self-sufficiency, a lone champion needing no one.

Both sides in disarming will have to stop lumping as "race" what is not racial:

The battle of the have vs. have nots—those who have homes and incomes vs. those who don't have.
The battle of the better educated vs. the poorer educated.
The battle of families with fathers present vs. fathers absent.

In the midst of a Civil War we need to

remember that you were at that time separated . . . you had no hope—no promise.[23]

Remembering at that time, Christ Jesus

designed to reconcile to God both Blacks and Whites in a single body by means of his cross, thus putting to death their hostility and bringing the feud to an end.[24] (Paraphrased)

The two, warring sides—once so far away—have been brought near by the work of Christ Jesus

in defeating Satan's invisible army,
in paying the war's costs by drinking the bitter cup of furies,
in healing the hate by taking the lashes on his own back,
in paying the price of Civil War blood spilled by shedding his own blood in payment of brother killing brother,
in offering both sides forgiveness to stitch up the open wounds,
in healing the sorrow with the balm of his love.

There is no other way. When blacks and whites accept the reconciling spirit and work of Christ in their lives, the battles will be over, the warfare ended.

For He is himself our peace. He has made both Blacks and Whites one body, one nation. He has broken down the hostile dividing wall between North and South. He abolished in his own crucified flesh the bitter antagonism caused by worldly laws and a worldly spirit that he from the two sides might create in himself one new person—one new quality of humanity out of the two— thereby making and bringing peace.[25] (Paraphrased)

The terms of peace have only to be accepted. The war is over; He has overcome.

Notes

1. Louis Meriwether, *Don't Ride the Bus on Monday: The Rosa Parks Story*, Prentice-Hall, Englewood Cliffs, N.J. 1973, (no page number).
2. Milton Viorst, *Fires in the Streets: America in the 1960s*, Simon and Schuster, New York, 1979, pp. 27–28.
3. Juan Williams, *Eyes on the Prize: America's Civil Rights Years*, 1954–1965, Viking Penguin, New York, 1987, p. 77.
4. Williams, p. 89.
5. Viorst, p. 34.
6. Viorst, p. 38. See p. 433.
7. Ella Baker in Williams, p. 137.
8. Viorst, pp. 118–119.
9. Williams, p. 174.
10. David Vann in Williams, p. 183.
11. SNCC (pronounced "snick") was the Student Nonviolent Coordinating Committee. The students led themselves.
12. Williams, p. 187.
13. Williams, p. 189.
14. 1 Corinthians 13:4. A telling verse for civil rights:

    Love (God's love in us) does not insist on its own rights or its own way, for it is not self-seeking; it is not touchy or fretful or resentful.

    —1 Corinthians 13:5 Amplified
15. **Supreme Court: Obey injunctions until they are set aside**

    [Justice] Black held sway in sustaining the convictions of Martin Luther King and other civil rights leaders for leading Easter Sunday protest marches in Birmingham, Alabama. The parade organizers were unable to get a permit, and they proceeded with their demonstration despite an injunction forbidding them to march without a permit. . . . Black countered, there was no excuse to violate an injunction. Clark, Stewart, and White supported Black immediately; Harlan demurred at first . . . [then] agreed the injunction should not have been ignored . . .

    Stewart's draft focused on the theme that people must obey injunctions until they succeed in having them set aside by a higher court. The draft ended by noting, "Patience is a small price for the civilizing hand of the judicial process, which alone can give abiding meaning to constitutional freedom." Stewart changed it to "a modicum of patience" and finally, to "respect for judicial process."

> —Bernard Schwartz with Stephan Lesher, *Inside the Warren Court*, Doubleday & Company, Garden City, New York, pp. 241–242.

16. Viorst, p. 331.
17. H. Rap Brown.
18. Thomas R. Brooks, *Walls Come Tumbling Down: A History of the Civil Rights Movement—1940–1970*, Prentice-Hall, Englewood Cliffs, NJ, 1947, pp. 262–265.
19. William T. Sherman.
20. Roy Wilkins in Brooks, p. 265.
21. **An end to scapegoating**
    - The fault, dear Brutus, is not in our stars,
      But in ourselves, that we are underlings.
      > —Shakespeare, *Julius Caesar*, I, ii, 139
    - Chiefly the mold of a man's fortune is in his own hands.
      > —Francis Bacon, *Essays*, "Of Fortune"
22. **An African-American Weekend**
    Forcing white and yellow people to bend the knee on the birthday of a black leader is not the way to peace. Wouldn't it be fairer to have an African-American Weekend celebrating the contributions of *all* Americans whose roots are in Africa? It might be the third weekend in August with Saturday celebrating secular contributions and Sunday lifting up the religious heritage. It wouldn't even have to be a national holiday to be joyful.
23. Ephesians 2:12 Amplified.
24. Ephesians 2:16 paraphrased.
25. Ephesians 2:14,15 paraphrased.

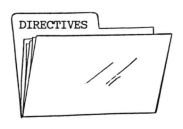

Anyone who has faith in me
   will do what I have been doing.
   He will do even greater things.
      —John 14:12 NIV

Directive: Spiritual Gifts are _Not_ for Today

TO:

1st Methodist	1st Southern Baptist
1st Presbyterian	1st Christian
1st Lutheran	1st Church of Christ
1st Congregational	1st Non-denominational
1st Baptist	1st All-denominational

Also, all saints Episcopal.

FROM: Denomination headquarters.

DIRECTIVE: Spiritual gifts are _not_ for today.[1] God showed his marvelous works to the early church—then withdrew them.

Wow! Hot off the line from denomination headquarters!—a directive declaring why First Churches don't have the nine spiritual gifts, the gifts of wisdom, knowledge, faith, healings, miracles, prophecy, discernment, speaking and interpreting tongues.[2] These gifts are not in First Churches because God

withdrew the gifts from the earth! The news traveled fast. The pastor told the administrator
  who told the chairperson of the board
  who told the secretary
  who told the bookkeeper
  who told the custodian
  who told the cook
  who blabbed it all over town: "No Christmas gifts this year!—or something like that."
Because the cook had trouble getting things right, she wrote the directive on one of her *From My Kitchen to Yours* cards. That night she handed it to the Spirit-filled preacher of the Church-on-Fire, where she went for evening praise services. The preacher wrote a reply:
"The hearts of some in the church have turned cold and lost the gifts, but, no, God has not withdrawn the gifts. A God who goes back on his word and takes back his gifts is not Scriptural:

> For God's gifts and His call are irrevocable—He never withdraws them when once they are given, and He does not change His mind about those to whom He gives His grace or to whom He sends His call.[3]

And Peter adds,

> The promise [the gift of the Holy Spirit] is for you and your children and for all who are far off."[4]

The preacher of the Church-on-Fire thought for a moment, then decided to add: *"far off* means in geography, into the Gentile world, and for years and centuries to come." With a satisfied nod of his head, the preacher gave the reply to the cook
  who gave it to the custodian
  who gave it to the bookkeeper
  who gave it to the secretary
  who gave it to the chairperson of the board

who gave it to the pastor

who gave it to headquarters—and headquarters was
  FURIOUS!

"Let's meet to draft a reply!" So sub-committee, committee, board, and president hammered out a pronouncement:

TO: All Churches.

FROM: Headquarters.

DIRECTIVE: *History* shows the spiritual gifts ended with the early church.

"Powerful!" thought the pastor of First Church as he told the administrator

who told the chairperson of the board

who told the secretary

who told the bookkeeper

who told the custodian

who told the cook

who gossiped all over town: "No shower gifts, either!—or
  something like that."

Again writing out the directive in pencil, she handed it to the Spirit-filled preacher who wrote out a reply:

"Not so, friends. History does not show the nine spiritual gifts ended—or even began—with the early church. The gifts have been here since day one. Here is a sketch of a gift that while controversial is also concrete: speaking a tongue, a language, that is not learned but given.

"History shows that when Adam and Eve were created, they didn't mumble

One grunt: water
Two grunts: food.

They were instantly given a 'tongue,' a language. It was Adam who named the animals:[5] hippopotamus, rhinoceros, armadillo. Tough words in any language.

"The Tower of Babel was built so high toward the clouds it caused the gift of tongues (languages) to be poured down from heaven. With speech confused, people had to seek out others who spoke and understood the same tongue.[6]

"King Saul spoke and sang in tongues, a language not learned but given, as he joined a group of ecstatic prophets.[7]

" 'This is the beginning of that!' rejoiced Peter at Pentecost. 'That which the prophet Joel spoke.' Fifteen known languages were spoken and recognized in Jerusalem that day.[8]

"In the 2nd century, revival of the gifts broke out. Tertullian and Irenaeus supported the awakening. In the 4th century, St. Augustine wrote, 'We still do what the apostles did . . . It is expected that converts should speak with new tongues.' In the 14th and 16th centuries, speaking in tongues was heard with St. Vincent Ferrer and St. Francis Xavier. Through the dark Middle Ages the Holy Spirit shone through the persecuted Waldenses and Albigenses—and the darkness could not put out the holy light.[9]

"The heavenly language continued through the Jansenists, the early Quakers, Shakers, and Methodists. In the 18th century, the early Methodists warmed the hearts of many as the fire of the Holy Spirit burned—causing sinners to tremble and fall down as dead, but being left with joy, divine dreams and visions.[10] The Holy Spirit moved on through the 'Irvingite' Church of the 19th century. Hearers of Dwight L. Moody were left on fire—and speaking in tongues and prophesying!

"On through Stone's Folly in Topeka, Kansas, and through an old livery stable on Azusa Street in the city of angels (*Los Angeles*) at the turn of the 1900s.[11] Light has been shining through the charismatics since the 1960s—and still the darkness has not stamped it out!

"Only a cold heart can dim the fire. Neither the Lord nor history has ended the gifts, and Satan can never put all of the gifts under a bushel."

The preacher handed the reply to the cook, and it soon found its way into the hands of headquarters. "OUTRAGEOUS!" they shouted. Subcommittee, committee, board, and president again wrenched out a decree.

> **DIRECTIVE:** The New Testament is completed; we now have the written word. No one needs the gifts of the Holy Spirit.

"But," simply replied the preacher of the Church-on-Fire, "what about the thorny issues of creating life in a test tube, abortion, mercy killing, unilateral disarmament, and chemical warfare—thorns which have no clear chapter and verse in the written word? Can we really say the modern world does not need help? . . . that we need no knowledge and wisdom from him in whom all wisdom dwells? . . . that we don't want the spiritual gifts of knowledge and wisdom shining through us, but would rather fumble along with earthly knowledge and earthly wisdom. No wonder Modern Times are a dark age of the spirit."

"REBEL!" thundered headquarters. They then issued the following:

> **DIRECTIVE:** When we release statements, the world knows they are true. We don't need signs and miracles following!

"Are all the people in the world Christian?" pondered the preacher in his reply. "Is there no longer darkness in famine-ridden Africa? Are there no longer occult spirits dancing across Brazil and South America? Are doors in the countries of Islam wide open to the gospel of peace? Or is it just that your pronouncements have not reached these far lands?

"Why should any people follow a dead Christianity? When the reverend of First Church preaches, few are saved. When he reads a prayer of healing, few are healed. When he reads a prayer of deliverance, the evil spirit replies: 'Jesus I know and Paul I know about, but who are you?'[12] Friends, no one is saved by a statement."[13]

Headquarters grew red in the face with fury. They RAGED as they wrote

> **DIRECTIVE:** If the gifts are for today, why don't we have them? We're the leaders!

"Yes . . ." worried the pastor of First Church, who was in charge of a dying flock. "Why are they—and why am I—so powerless?" The pastor told the administrator
who slowly told the chairperson of the board
who slowly told the secretary
who slowly told the bookkeeper
who slowly told the custodian
who slowly told the cook— who finally got it right.

The preacher quietly wrote his reply: " 'According to your faith let it be done to you.'[14] An open hand receives, a closed hand holding on to church power receives nothing. For Christ to live, leaders must die at the Cross.

"Some leaders at headquarters fear the spiritual. You cannot control it. You are afraid of being deceived. But to reject the working of the Holy Spirit because there is a counterfeit Angel of Light at work in the world is like rejecting Christ because there is an anti-Christ. It is rejecting the Bible because there are other 'sacred' writings. It is rejecting church because there are cults. Rejecting love because there is hurt. Rejecting marriage because there is divorce. Rejecting living because there is dying.

"Yet we are not left orphans. Cheer up!"

Headquarters looked long and hard at the reply. "We underestimated the simple preacher," they agreed. With a heavy spirit—"under conviction" the preacher would say—the subcommittee, committee, board, and president wearily met. Holding on to their doctrine with dying breath, they uttered,

> **DIRECTIVE:** We have Christ. That's all we need.

The brokenhearted pastor told the brokenhearted administrator
  who told the brokenhearted chairperson of the board
  who told the brokenhearted secretary
  who told the brokenhearted bookkeeper
  who told the brokenhearted custodian
  who told the brokenhearted cook
  who confessed it tearfully all over town: "Not only will there
    be no gifts this year, but there will be no love, no joy, no
    peace, no kindness[15] . . . No Spirit . . ." she sobbed.

As she wrote out the message on her recipe card, a tear fell,
smearing the pencil mark and staining the card. She gave the
card to the Spirit-filled preacher, who wrote his reply.

"You say, 'Christ is all we need.' For salvation, yes. But what
about the Father, who is Creator and Master Designer? What
about the Holy Spirit with his fruit, gifts, and holiness? No, the
three Persons in one work together and 'need' each other.
Christ Jesus pointed beyond himself to the other two Persons:

> The Father is greater and mightier than I am. The Father Who
> lives continually in Me does the works—His miracles, His own
> deeds of power.
>
> The Comforter (Counselor, Helper, Intercessor, Advocate,
> Strengthener, Standby), the Holy Spirit, Whom the Father will
> send in My name [in My place, to represent Me and act on My
> behalf], He will teach you all things.[16]

Headquarters met. The committee said, "If there is more of
the Holy Spirit out there than we got at the time of salvation,
we don't want to find ourselves opposing God." The Board nodded, "Let's watch the Spirit-filled churches to see if they have a
power that we don't."

Feeling more hopeful, the president picked up his file folder
and rose. As he was about to suggest they adjourn for lunch, a
recipe card fell from among the papers he had that day put into
his file folder.

"What's this?" he wondered, picking up the card from the floor. The heading on the card read: *From My Kitchen to Yours.*

Why can't the lifestyles be many and the Spirit one?[17]
Then we can all have Gifts.

— The Cook

"That's it?" cried the president, elated.

"That's it!" cried the board.

"That's it!" cried the pastor of First Church a week later, holding in his hand the latest word from headquarters. It read:

> **DIRECTIVE:** Let the lifestyles be many, but the Spirit one. (And give your cook a hug!)

Notes

1. Many insights on spiritual gifts being for today are from Donald Gee, *Concerning Spiritual Gifts*, Gospel Publishing House, Springfield, Missouri, "Are Spiritual Gifts for Today?" pp. 18–22.
2. 1 Corinthians 12:4–11.
3. Romans 11:29 Amplified.
4. Acts 2:39 NIV.
   Gifts needed on earth to get the job done
   > He said to them, "Go into all the world and preach the good news to all creation. And these signs will accompany those who believe: In my name they will drive out demons; they will speak in new tongues . . . they will place their hands on sick people, and they will get well."
   >
   > After the Lord Jesus had spoken to them, he was taken up into heaven and he sat at the right hand of God. Then the disciples went out and preached everywhere, and the Lord worked with them and confirmed his word by the signs that accompanied it.
   >
   > —Mark 16:15,17–20 NIV. See Hebrews 2:4.

   How long will we need gifts like knowledge, tongues, and prophecy? Until the end of life on earth. They will then cease, for at that time we will see things perfectly and face to face. (See 1 Corinthians 13:8–12)
5. Genesis 2:20.
6. Genesis 11:1–9.
7. Genesis 10:1–13. "Prophesied ecstatically" (v. 10) in Smith-Goodspeed. "Inspired speaking" (v. 13) in Amplified. Compare with "drunk with wine" in Acts 2:1–18.
8. Acts 2:1–18 Amplified.
9. John L. Sherrill, *They Speak with Other Tongues*, Pyramid Publications, New York, 1964, pp. 76–78 and Gee, pp. 19–20.
10. *The Journal of John Wesley,* Moody Press, Chicago, pp. 76, 99, 239.
11. Sherrill, pp. 33–43.

12. Acts 19:15 NIV.

13.   For the kingdom of God is not a matter of talk but of power.
       —1 Corinthians 4:20 NIV. See 1 Corinthians
       2:4,5.

14. Matthew 9:29 New RSV.

15. Galatians 5:22, 23.

16. John 14:28b, 10b, 26 Amplified.

17.   Let us therefore stop turning critical eyes on one another. If
       we must be critical, let us be critical of our own conduct and
       see that we do nothing to make a brother stumble or fall. It is
       to God alone that we have to answer for our actions. So open
       your hearts to one another as Christ has opened his heart to
       you, and God will be glorified.
       —Romans 14:13,12; 15:7 Phillips. See 14:1 to
       15:7.

As Peter entered the house,
Cornelius met him and fell
at his feet in reverence.
But Peter made him get up.
"Stand up," he said, "I am
only a man myself."
—Acts 10:25–26 NIV

A Visit from the Pope

IMAGINE an ordinary family in twentieth century America. Now imagine them having a visit from the first pope, the apostle Peter himself. What would Peter say? What would happen?

King's Corner was buzzing all day. "We're just an average American town," said one awed woman. "Yet Peter is coming here . . ."

"It's because we're ordinary he's coming," remarked her companion.

Photographers and TV crews had descended on King's Port, a coastal community near San Diego. They waited in vans and mobile units parked outside the home of Cornelius and Dolores Rivera.[1]

Cornelius was a police officer. Not the chief, just . . . an officer. A devout and kindly man, he was well-liked. He even gave a tithe to his church: St. Peter's.

"I don't see him," worried Rhoda, peeking through the front curtains. Rhoda was seven-years-old and . . . well, let's say "lively."

"He'll come," reassured Dolores, forgetting what she was going for and then, with a shrug, returning to her former spot.

"In a popemobile?!" eagerly asked Rhoda.

"Of course," calmly replied Cornelius. "It was specially built for him." Cornelius was immensely proud of the pope visiting his home—yet not *too* proud.

There was knocking at the door. The back door. "You expecting someone to drop over?" asked Dolores.

"Only if his name is Peter," joked Cornelius. Dolores smiled. "Rhoda, see who's at the back door."

"Me?! Why me? I'll miss the pope!"

"Go answer the back door," distinctly repeated Dolores.

"Oh-h-h-h." Flipping the curtain back in place, Rhoda dashed to the back door, flung it open, tossed out a "Hi!" and scampered back to her lookout at the front window.

"Who was it?" inquired Cornelius.

"I don't know. An old guy."

"An old man?" Puzzled, Dolores straightened her dress before seeing who it was.

"With whiskers."

"Oh, Rhoda," cautioned Cornelius, rising. "Tell us right off if a stranger comes to the house."

Meanwhile, the bewhiskered old man remained standing before the wide-open door.

Dolores stepped aside, letting Cornelius handle the matter. *Homeless*, she thought. Then she remembered some cold cuts in the refrigerator that would make a nice snack for a work-for-food transient.

"Yes?" inquired Cornelius.

"I'm Peter. I think maybe you're waiting for me."

Cornelius's eyes widened. His mouth fell open. Falling at the feet of Peter, he grasped Peter's hand and kissed it.

"Stop it, man," Peter said half humorously, half scoldingly. "I'm a common man just like you.[2] Get up," he continued, helping Cornelius to his feet.

"But . . . The back door?"

"Too many people out front. I'm here to visit you, not them. Besides, what I do in secret the Lord will reward openly."

"But the Vatican's press and photographers . . . "

"Aaagh. I pay them no mind. You can't catch fish with all that folderol. Quietness—that's the secret."

"I guess maybe you're right . . ." Peter—*this* Peter—isn't what Cornelius expected.

"Please," said a respectful Dolores. "Won't you come into the living room?"

"Why not," Peter said with gusto. Boldly he strode into the living room. Dolores scurried after him. "Rhoda, this is our visitor: Peter."

"HIM?!" Rhoda was shocked. Turning, Rhoda looked out the window for what she had missed. Then she turned toward Peter. "Where's your popemobile?"

Peter laughed heartily. "I'm a fisherman. I own a fishing boat. That's all."

"But . . . But." Disappointment spread like wrinkles across Rhoda's face. Such a down-and-out pope! No robe, no ring, no—Nothing.

"Please," smiled Dolores. "Won't you sit?" Dolores indicated the overstuffed chair, which for this occasion had a covering of embroidered church crosses.

"Thank you," replied Peter. "But what are all these?"

"Crosses," smiled Dolores. She pointed them out. "The Canterbury and Celtic. The crosses of Lorraine and Iona. Here's a Fleurée; there's a Patée. In the center . . ." Dolores swelled with pride. "Just for you, the Papal cross! I looked them all up," she beamed.

"Where . . ." Peter squinted, trying to find what he was looking for. "Where's the wooden cross of Jesus?"

"If you look real close, you can see a hint of it in each one. We . . ." Dolores blushed. "We call it . . . *Peter's Chair.*"

"Hmmm." Looking around, Peter caught sight of a simple dining room chair. "Mind if I sit on this?" He forthrightly turned the chair around. "It's wood. I'm a fisherman, and I sit on wood in my boat." He smiled broadly as his body sat on good ol' comfortable wood.

Rhoda had a mischievous glint in her eye. Walking up to Peter, she said straightforwardly, "My best friend is Protestant." Dolores gasped. Cornelius looked heavenward, wondering if they sent him the right child.

"Good," replied Peter. "As long as your friend loves and walks with God and is kind to people, your friend will be welcomed by the Master."[3]

Dolores glared at him. "What you say your name was?"

"Peter."

"I believe you're right," said Cornelius sincerely. "I've always felt it was a matter of the heart and of searching out the will of God that counted."

"That's why I was sent to your house," said Peter matter-of-factly. "You're a good man, Cornelius."

Hearing Peter leave her out of the compliment, Dolores heaved her chest indignantly. And in her house! Suspicious of this man, Dolores thought she'd better get to the bottom of things. "Your name is *Peter*? As in *Pope* Peter?"

"Goodness, no. I've been called hot-tempered, but never 'pope.' "

"It's Latin—I think," added Dolores.

"I don't know Latin. You don't need Latin to catch fish," laughed Peter lustily. Dolores just blinked. Rhoda had edged closer again during the conversation. "But you are a pope . . . a *real* pope, aren't you?"

Peter shook his head. "There are no popes in the Bible. Just carpenters and tax collectors. And fishermen!" he added brightly.

Pouting, Rhoda turned away. "No wonder they never gave *him* a popemobile . . ."

"But . . ." Cornelius was confused. "You *are* the Rock, aren't you?"

"No, no, no, no. Christ is the Rock.[4] My name is Peter, meaning *rock*, but the living Rock, the Rock of all ages is

Christ. He was the Rock before I was born. He'll be the Rock after the world passes away. No . . . I'm a part of his rock, but you don't build a church on a chip but on the *whole* rock. My friends John and Paul are part of the same rock. It's the Rock of Christ that the power of Death will not prevail against."

"I don't understand." Cornelius was deeply puzzled. Peter felt it was time to get down to business. "When Jesus died, Hades wanted him. But Jesus rose on Easter, and with him, the church. The gates of Hades had to close—empty."

Peter saw Cornelius still trying to put things together in his mind. Peter went on. "When the twelve disciples die, the church does not die with them, it lives on through those who are saved, those added to their number day by day. When that generation dies, another generation of believers becomes the body through which Christ lives. When the Middle Ages pass, the gates of Hades still cannot shut down the church. When the Age of Reason dies, when the Modern Age passes away . . . what will remain?" Peter waited for an answer. Cornelius looked at Dolores; Dolores cast her eyes down, not knowing.

"The church!" called out Peter. "The Living Rock! CHRIST!"

The picture Cornelius had of the church was still out of focus. "But . . . The keys of the kingdom, they're yours . . ."

"No, no, no. Look at it this way: When the Master was about to return to heaven, he handed the keys of the kingdom to his servants.[5] The keys were not given away for keeps, but only until a servant finished his work. Then the keys return to the Master. If a servant doesn't want to return the keys, the power of the keys *still* returns to the Master." Peter then added with a shake of the head, "Replica keys have no power.

"The reason keys are handed to servants is that they might open the store room and provide food for the world.[6] The keys are spiritual. The food is spiritual. The servants are answerable at all times to the Master of the house. The keys are his. The house is his. The world is his! 'My church,'[7] Jesus said simply."

"There's more than one key," remarked Cornelius thoughtfully.

"My, yes! At the proper time, the Master gives a key to a servant he has called, to a servant who has received gifts of the Spirit. Without the gifts, there's no way you can get the work done! I used one of my keys to open the door to a house on Pentecost, so Jews could be filled with the Holy Spirit.[8] Then I used a second key to open the door to a house of another fellow named Cornelius, opening the kingdom to the Gentiles.[9]

"Paul used a key to unlock mysteries as he revealed mighty truths in writing letters. He used another key to unlock prisons.

"Martin Luther used a key to Castle Church to bind the dark ages of Christendom and loosen learning. Now there's a man I like—Luther! Boldest man since . . . well, since *me!*"

Peter's robust laugh punctured the timid air. He resumed. "John Wesley used his key to enter a house on Aldersgate Street, loosening a warm Spirit upon a frozen church. And *that's* how the Master has used his keys through the ages, giving the right keys to the right servants."

"But . . . The popes!" Dolores was aghast. "*You didn't mention the popes!*"

"Man-made. Something the Roman church made up along the way. If a godly man is pope, he'll be saved because he's a godly man—not because he's pope. Now if you want to follow the keys through the centuries, look to where the Holy Spirit is bearing fruit. *That's* where the living Christ is! *That's* where the keys to the kingdom are! Opening and shutting." Peter gave a definitive nod of his head. *Not badly said, for a fisherman,* he thought.

Dolores sank into the over-stuffed chair—between the Canterbury and Fleurée crosses. "If the priest ever knew," she thought. "*Ai-y-y-y!*"

Just then a wind blew through the house. "Rhoda!" called out Dolores. "Close the window!"

"But . . . it *is* closed." Rhoda was perplexed, the wind stirring her hair.

"Then the door, close it!" Dolores felt the wind flush against her face.

"But the door . . . is closed, too."

"Here we go again!" roared Peter joyfully.[10] "Let 'er rip, Lord! The whole gale!"

Cornelius, amazed, rose to his feet. No sooner had he risen than he fell backwards—like a cedar of Lebanon being cut down that the Temple might be built up.

"Wow!" cried Rhoda, excited. "Can I do that?"

"Why not?" Peter extended his hand toward the girl. Smoothly, Rhoda fell backwards, like a long-stemmed rose being laid on an altar.

Dolores stood, her heart overflowing with gladness. "This Peter is real. He's brought the power of God!" Looking heavenward, Dolores cried aloud, "Me, too. Don't forget me, Lord!" Arms outstretched, Dolores fell backwards, leaning softly into the everlasting arms of God.

Peter smiled. There lying on the floor, hands open to receive, were three people with the faith of babies talking to their daddy. All were praising God in a language they never learned. Dolores and Rhoda repeated words, magnifying God. While their words were limited, their heart to heart talk with the Father was limitless. Rhoda spoke Chinese. Dolores, Latin. Cornelius—ah, it was nice to hear Aramaic again. Spoken fluently!

As they spoke, the Holy Spirit presented their deepest desires and thoughts before the Father.[11] Then the Holy Spirit turned to face the family as each family member received God's reply.

His work done, Peter quietly left. By the back door.

Notes

1. Acts 10.
2. **What the Bible says about bowing down before another person and paying homage to him**

   As Peter arrived, Cornelius met him, and falling down at his feet he made obeisance and paid worshipful reverence to him. But Peter raised him up, saying, Get up; I myself am also a man.

   —Acts 10:25,26 Amplified

   Compare this with the coronation of a pope today:

   He sits on a portable throne and is carried in a procession from the Vatican to the place of his coronation. . . . At the coronation site, the cardinals pay homage to the pope by bowing before him and kissing his foot. The pope then says Mass.

   —Fulton J. Sheen, "Pope," *The World Book Encyclopedia*, 1978, P, Vol. 15, p. 590.

   Ezekiel's prophecy against the King of Tyre:

   The word of the LORD came to me: "Son of man, say to the ruler of Tyre, 'This is what the Sovereign LORD says:

   " 'In the pride of your heart
   you say, "I am a god;
   I sit on the throne of a god
   in the heart of the seas."
   But you are a man and not a god . . ."

   —Ezekiel 28:1,2 NIV

   The book of Esther:

   All the royal officials at the kings gate knelt down and paid honor to Haman, for the king had commanded this concerning him. But Mordecai would not kneel down or pay him honor.

   When Haman saw that Mordecai would not kneel down or pay him honor, he was enraged.

   —Esther 3:2,5 NIV

   From John the apostle:

   I, John, am the one who heard and saw these things. And when I had heard and seen them, I fell down to worship at the feet of the angel who had been showing them to me. But he said to me, "Do not do it! I am a fellow servant with you and with your brothers the prophets and of all who keep the words of this book. Worship God!"

—Revelation 22:8,9 NIV

3. And Peter opened his mouth and said: Most certainly and thoroughly I now perceive and understand that God shows no partiality and is no respecter of persons, But in every nation he who venerates and has a reverential fear of God, treating Him with worshipful obedience and living uprightly, is acceptable to him and sure of being received and welcomed [by Him].

—Acts 10:34,35 Amplified. "No partiality" in Deuteronomy 10:7, Romans 2:11, Ephesians 6:9, and Colossians 3:25.

The prophet Micah sounds the same note as Peter:

He has showed you, O man, what is good;
and what does the LORD require of you
but to do justice, and to love kindness,
and to walk humbly with your God?

—Micah 6:8 RSV

4. **What the Bible says about Christ being the Rock**
A Song of Moses:

I will proclaim the name of the LORD.
Oh, praise the greatness of our God!
He is the Rock, his works are perfect.
Jeshurun grew fat and kicked;
He abandoned the God who made him
and rejected the Rock his Savior.
You deserted the Rock, who fathered you;
you forgot the God who gave you birth.

The LORD will judge his people
and have compassion on his servants.
He will say: "Now where are their gods,
the rock they took refuge in,
the gods who ate the fat of their sacrifices?"

For their rock is not like our Rock.

—Deuteronomy 32:3,4,15,18,36–38,31. Condensed from NIV.

A Psalm of David:

> My soul finds rest in God alone;
> my salvation comes from him.
> He alone is my rock and my salvation.
> —Psalm 62:1,2 NIV

Isaiah:

> So trust in the Lord—commit yourself to Him, lean on Him, hope confidently in Him—for ever; for the Lord God is an everlasting rock—the Rock of ages.
> —Isaiah 26:4 Amplified

> "This is what the LORD says—
> Who then is like me? Is there any God besides me?
> No, there is no other Rock; I know not one."
> —Isaiah 44:6–8 NIV condensed

Paul writing about Israel's history:

> They were all baptized into Moses in the cloud and in the sea. They all ate the same spiritual food and drank the same spiritual drink; for they drank from the spiritual rock that accompanied them, and that rock was Christ.
> —1 Corinthians 10:2–4 NIV

Jesus:

> You are Peter [petros, masculine, a large piece of rock], and on this rock [petra, feminine, a huge rock like Gibraltar] I will build My church . . .
> —Matthew 16:18 Amplified

5. **What the Bible says about** *all* **the disciples being given the keys of the kingdom** (emphasis added)

At that time the disciples came to Jesus . . .

Jesus taught them:

> "I tell you the truth, whatever you bind on earth will be bound in heaven, and whatever you loose on earth will be loosed in heaven."
> —Matthew 18:1,18 NIV

On the evening of that first day of the week, when the disciples were together, with the doors locked for fear of the Jews, Jesus came and stood among them and said, "Peace be with you!" After he said this, he showed them his hands and side. The disciples were overjoyed when they saw the Lord.

Again Jesus said, "Peace be with you! As the Father has sent me, I am sending you." And with that he breathed on *them* and said, "Receive the Holy Spirit. If you forgive anyone his sins, they are forgiven; if you do not forgive them, they are not forgiven."

—John 20:19–23 NIV

You are built upon the foundation of the apostles and prophets . . .

—Ephesians 2:20 Amplified

And the wall of the city had twelve foundation [stones], and on them the twelve names of the twelve apostles of the Lamb.

—Revelation 21:14 Amplified

6. Many insights on keys of the kingdom come from Matthew Henry, *A Commentary on the Whole Bible,* Vol. 5, *Matthew to John,* World Bible Publishers, Iowa Falls, Iowa, pp. 232–234.
7. Matthew 16:18.
8. Acts 2.
9. Acts 10.
10. Acts 2.
11. Romans 8:26–27.

Even the stork in the sky
knows her appointed seasons,
and the dove, the swift and the thrush
observe the time of their migration.
—Jeremiah 8:7 NIV

The Stork Knows the Season

EVEN the stork in the sky knows the time to build a nest and the time to fly south. The stork knows the seasons—and doesn't even consult a calendar! How is this done? By the stork being attuned to the seasons of the spirit on the level where creatures live and the Holy Spirit ("Mother Nature") directs.

Did you know there are spiritual seasons? On the higher levels, these are seasons in the spirit realm where God, Satan, and the human spirit live, move and have their being. What happens in the spirit realm may express itself openly in the earthly realm.

Thumbnail sketches of spiritual seasons seen on earth might be: Summer is arguing with a neighbor, autumn is building a fence, winter is not speaking, spring is lending the neighbor a hand. On the job, summer is a treadmill, autumn manipulation, winter quitting, spring a promotion. In battle, summer is courage, autumn retreat, winter defeat, spring is victory.

Eyes are blazing in summer, dim in autumn, blind in winter, bright in spring. Hearts are passionate in summer, cool in autumn, cold in winter, warm in spring. Summer is facing a person, autumn facing self, winter facing Satan, spring facing

177

God. Spiritually, summer is growing, autumn dying, winter death, spring birth.

Earthly seasons follow the same order—summer, autumn, winter, spring—because the earth is titled and revolves around the sun. The earth has physical seasons, following laws that God laid down when he formed the foundation of the world.

Spiritual seasons do not have to follow any order. It is God who controls the seasons of the spirit just as he controls where the wind blows, where the wind starts, and where the wind finishes. Some gusts are short, others long. God has the final word on how long seasons of the spirit last.

There is not one spiritual season at a time. Seasons of the spirit come in layers. The whole history of the world might be seen as spring (creation), summer (people rebelling/returning), autumn (a falling away), winter (the coldness of the last days), ending with spring (the reign of Christ). In between there are untold seasons. If there were to be but one season spanning the layers below it, that season would be spring, for first and last God poured out his love upon his creation, upon his sons and daughters.

In the life of Esther, there was a season of spring (becoming queen), winter (isolated, not seeing the king), summer (confronting Haman at dinner), autumn (people siding with Haman's sons), summer (the battles with the Persians), and spring (God turning a day of sorrow into gladness). On a higher layer sweeping over these gusts of the spirits was an overarching wind of one season: spring, for God was doing a mighty act in delivering his people Israel.

Jesus talked about spiritual seasons when he talked about the last days. We are able to see these seasons appearing throughout earth's history. Here is a closer look at each season.

Summer

The spiritual season of summer is marked by battles. It is a time when God's mighty army fights with Satan's troops. A time when the going is tough for people, when we have to battle every inch of the way, when nothing comes easy. The going is hard in the home, on the job, and in the world at large. There may be progress, stalemate, or defeat. Whatever, it is a struggle.

> For nation will rise against nation,
> and kingdom against kingdom. [1]

In the spiritual season of summer, where will the battles be? In Jericho, a walled city. In the Valley of Elah, where Goliath waits. In Persia, where Haman casts lots. In Babylon, where a furnace burns seven times hotter than usual. In Tours, France, where Moslems with swords drawn are invading.

Where will the battles be fought? At Yorktown, where redcoats have crossed the ocean. "Over there"—where going over the top on the western front is anything but quiet. At Pearl Harbor, where modern samurais swat ships to the bottom of the sea. On Mount Suribachi, where an American flag is raised on volcanic ash. In the Ardennes Forest, where an offer of surrender is answered, "Nuts."

> And there will be famines and earthquakes in place after place. [2]

In summer. Famines in India and Africa. Earthquakes in Lisbon and San Francisco.

> Then they will hand you over to suffer affliction and tribulation, and put you to death; and you will be hated by all nations for My name's sake. [3]

We may be blinded like Samson, yet out hair will grow back and our strength will return. We may be stoned like Stephen, yet through the flurry of rocks we will see Jesus standing at the right hand of God. We may be torn by lions in Rome, yet a letter sent to us will shape the world. We may be burned at the stake like John Huss, yet the flames may one day burn away the blindness of those who set the fire. All in the spiritual season of summer.

Even in a season of battles there are lulls, moments of quiet, moments of rest and fun. Summer has time for re-creation, for God is still the God of life.

Autumn

Summer may blend into autumn. Autumn is a time of cooling off, of falling away, of backsliding. It is a time of leaving convictions and beliefs behind, of being pragmatic. It is living by our wits, of playing the game the way the world plays it. Ethics depend on the situation, what we can get away with. Autumn is "practical." It is taking matters into our own hands, believing in *numero uno.*

> And then many will be offended and repelled and begin to distrust and desert (Him Whom they ought to trust and obey) and will stumble and fall away, and betray one another and pursue one another with hatred. And many false prophets will rise up and deceive and lead many into error.[4]

Autumn is an in-between season. It may be a reaction to the hard-fought battles of summer as the pendulum swings back, no longer outgoing, but inward-looking. No longer are we fighting for others; we are taking care of ourselves.

In autumn "many will fall away." Lot's wife, who couldn't keep her eyes off Sodom. A generation of Israelites, who couldn't keep their eyes off the Golden Calf. Saul, who looked to the witch of Endor for help. A rich, young ruler, who couldn't keep his eyes off his money. Churchgoers, whose eyes see science as savior in an age of reason.

Falling away in autumn are young men and women from Christian homes who are shacked up ("living together"), fornicating ("seeing if we're compatible"), adulterers ("swinging . . .

ours is an open marriage"), into orgies ("experimenting a lit-tle . . . trying new techniques"), addicted to drugs ("having a little high now and then"), and having abortions ("a baby's not convenient right now").

In autumn "many will betray one another." Delilah with questions. Judas with a kiss. A youth with a word, as he turns in his Lutheran parents to the Nazis. A preacher, with snapshots of another preacher secretly rendezvousing at a motel.

In autumn "many will hate each other." As the Inquisitor hates and tortures those who disagree with him. As the Ana-baptists are hated for wanting to baptize only adult believers.

In autumn "many false prophets will rise up and deceive and lead many into error." Voices—deceiver and deceived alike—echo through the centuries:

> "If the radiance of a thousand suns were to burst forth at once in the sky, that would be like the splendor of the Mighty One (Krishna)."[5]

> "Our god, Dagon, has delivered Samson into our hands!"[6]

> "O Baal, answer us!"[7]

> "I go for refuge to the Buddha."[8]

> "There is no god but Allah."[9]

> "Jesus is not Lord, not God, not Messiah, not Virgin-born. One God, not the Trinity."[10]

> "When our father Adam came into the Garden of Eden, he came into it with a celestial body and brought Eve, one of his celestial wives . . ."[11] And: "The son of God cometh upon the face of the earth. And behold, he shall be born of Mary, at Jerusalem . . ."[12]

> "Only 144,000 will reign!"[13]

> "Disease is error. Death an illusion."[14]

> "Workers of the world, unite!"[15]

> "Heil, Hitler!"

ED FISCHER
Courtesy Omaha World-Herald

"The goddess is alive—magic is afoot!"[16]

"O-m-m-m-m-m!"[17]

Not all turning needs to be turning away. There is beauty in a leaf turning from green to red to flame. There is also beauty in a heart turning to God. Crisp air may awaken our flesh on earth. A crisp season may awaken our souls to know our time is short. In autumn.

Winter

Autumn may weave into winter. Winter is the season of the cold heart.

> "Because of the increase of wickedness, the love of most will grow cold."
> "So when you see standing in the holy place 'the abomination that causes desolation,' spoken of through the prophet Daniel—let the reader understand—then let those who are in Judea flee to the mountains. Let no one on the roof of his house go down to take anything out of the house. Let no one in the field go back to get his cloak. How dreadful it will be in those days for pregnant women and nursing mothers! Pray that your flight will not take place in the winter . . . [18]

Guess the following period of history:

> The earth was depraved and putrid in God's sight, and the land was filled with violence (desecration, infringement, outrage, assault, and lust for power).[19]

Read your morning newspaper for more details. In addition, the words can apply to Noah's Day (the above quote), Babylon, the decline of Rome, the Dark Ages, and chunks of recent centuries when people walked in great darkness. Winter is a time of not caring; a cold heart doesn't care.

Winter is Laban. He pretended to give Jacob a bride of Rachel, but beneath the veil was Leah. He treated Jacob as a slave, not family. Laban coldly stole spotted goats and black lambs and changed Jacob's wages ten times that Jacob might be poor.

Winter is Pharisees. When Jesus healed a withered hand on the Sabbath, the only thing religious rulers could see was a man-made rule of "working" on the Sabbath broken. They could not see a healed, restored, waving, joyful hand! When Jesus healed, the Pharisees plotted the murder of Jesus—both on that Sabbath day.

> Woe to you, teachers of the law and Pharisees, you hypocrites! You are like whitewashed tombs, which look beautiful on the outside but on the inside are full of dead men's bones and everything unclean. In the same way, on the outside you appear to people as righteous but on the inside you are full of hypocrisy and wickedness. [20]

Winter is popery. It is Pope Alexander VI, the father of six, [21] who got tired of hearing God's prophet cry out, "At St. Peter's the whores go in and out!"[22] Yet it was more for political reasons that Pope Alexander had a hand in murdering this prophet. [23] Winter is Pope Sergius III, who marched on Rome with armed men. Afterwards—when he looked into the prison—he saw there two popes who wanted his throne. He had them both strangled to death. [24] Winter is John XII, who committed incest (sleeping with his sisters), who drank toasts to the devil, and who, caught in the act of adultery, had his skull bashed in with a hammer by the enraged husband. [25]

Winter is the Political Church, political not because it takes a stand on social issues, but because it is run like a secular corporation. There are bureaucrats, committees, human reason, human will, and human power plays. It is a liberal church—centered on John and Jane Doe and run by John and Jane Doe. It is a clay church, earthbound. It is a frozen church, cold to God.

The large, double doors of the Political Church open like doors to a solemn tomb. The people enter, sensing a deadness. They feel a chill, for they have entered the season of winter. Their souls cry out for a touch of God, a healing, a quickening of the spirit! But the spirit of Death passes over. They have joined their bodies to a cold body. Souls sitting in these frozen churches are feeling the frost of that most terrible winter.

In winter, the battle of the sexes is a cold war. Women look at men and accuse them of being "lazy, lustful, and self-centered."[26] *Lazy* because they talk about a man helping with the housework—but don't lift a finger to do it. It is the wife who comes home from her job place to a second shift of diapers and dishes. *Lustful* because a woman feels when a man meets her he is thinking, "I wonder how good she is in bed?" *Self-centered* because he feels only his opinion matters in world affairs—and sports.

The man, for his part, feels his woman is not there for him. A wife at the office is away from home, husband, and kids. A wife fulfilling herself is doing it at the cost of leaving her man empty. Both want to believe the cold war is because things are the way they are—a social problem, nothing more. Yet nagging at their souls is a question: Isn't the coldness the cold of winter?

Winter is the Soviet Union stripping Eastern Europe of her dignity, her freedom, her factories and bread. It is jailing the Hungarian church of Cardinal Mindszenty for "treason." Winter is Communist tanks rolling in from the Soviet Union to crush Hungarians in the streets for believing Hungary belongs to Hungarians.[27]

Winter is 800,000 Communist boots marching into Czechoslovakia to crush the flower of freedom.[28] It is Soviet tanks in the streets of Prague. It is the paw of a Soviet Bear on the shoulder of Czech press, radio and television—until one day the Czechs are caged in a zoo with the Soviet Bear on the outside holding the keys.

Winter is Poland's Communist prison of police power, controlled elections, and a constitution "printed in the Soviet Union." It is Polish land farmed with a hammer and sickle.

Winter is Russian poets shivering in Siberian exile. Cold Wars belong to winter.

Even in the season of winter, we are not abandoned. Looking out on a whitened landscape, we may feel serene, for just as snowflakes fall gently, so does the grace of God fall upon the earth. Even in our dying, Christ stands beside us. No matter how deep the grave, the arms of God are deeper still to cradle us.

Spring

Spring is the season of God's power breaking through. It is victory, rebirth, and celebration.

> They will see the Son of man coming out on the clouds of heaven with power and great glory—in brilliancy and splendor. And He will send out His angels with a loud trumpet call, and they will gather His elect [His chosen ones] from the four winds, [even] from one end of the universe to the other.[29]

Spring is each of the seven days of creation. It is Ruth. It is Elijah's mantle. It is Esther coming to the kingdom for such a time as this. It is Job declaring, "I have seen things too wonderful for words." It is David writing the Psalms.

Spring is the words of a wise man. It is Solomon's temple. It is Hosea going in search of his wandering Gomer. It is Joel prophesying, "I will pour out my Spirit upon all people." It is Micah's insightful, "What does the Lord require of you but to do justice, and to love kindness, and to walk humbly with your God."

Spring is Christmas, not a gift of straw, but a Lamb. It is Easter, a stony heart rolled away. Spring is being newborn in the Spirit and speaking words not learned but given by a heavenly

Father. Spring is leaping and praising God at the gate Beautiful. It is the Lamb upon his throne!

Spring is a ceiling painted in the Sistine Chapel. It is posting 95 beliefs on the door of a church. It is Frances of Assisi loving creatures. It is John Wesley at a quarter of nine: "I felt my heart strangely warmed." It is J.S. Bach writing "Jesu, Joy of Man's Desiring." It is Handel echoing, "Halleluia!"

Spring is setting foot on Ellis island. It is the eleventh hour of the eleventh month: armistice. It is the good ship Lollipop. The good ship Hope. A polka from Czechoslovakia, a waltz from Vienna. It is an outpouring of the Holy Spirit creating Christian radio and television, songs and literature. It is Eastern Europeans taking to the streets and shouting: "Open the Wall!" "Free elections!" "To the castle!" Very simply, spring is God sending his love to the hearts of his children!

Notes

1. Matthew 24:7.
2. Matthew 24:7.
3. Matthew 24:9.
4. Matthew 24:10,11.
5. *Bhagavad Gita*, chapter 11, verse 12. A sacred writing in Hinduism. Krishna is one of the Hindu gods.
6. See Judges 16:23.
7. 1 Kings 18:26.
8. A traditional liturgy in Buddhism.
9. A creed in Islam.
10. See Walter R. Martin, *The Kingdom of the Cults*, Bethany Fellowship, Inc., Minneapolis, Minnesota, 1965, "Unitarianism," pp. 425–26.
11. Mormon leader Brigham Young in Martin, p. 178. But Adam and Eve did not "come" to the Garden like star trekkers. In Eden, Adam and Eve were created, had the breath of life breathed into them, and became living beings for the first and only time. (Genesis 2:7, 21–24)
12. Born in "Bethlehem" according to Matthew 2:1 and Micah 5:2. Quote from the *Book of Mormon* (Alma 7:9,10) in Martin, pp. 166–167.
13. See Martin, "Jehovah's Witnesses and the Watch Tower," pp. 50, 97–98, 106.
14. See Martin, "Christian Science and New Thought," pp. 116, 123.
15. Karl Marx and Friedrich Engels, *The Communist Manifesto*.
16. In Naomi R. Goldenberg, *Changing of the Gods: Feminism and the End of Traditional Religions*, Beacon Press, Boston, 1979, p. 92.
17. New Age chant.
18. Matthew 24:12, 15–20 NIV.
19. Genesis 6:11.
20. Matthew 23:27,28 NIV.

21. "At least six" in Eric John (ed.), *The Popes*, Hawthorn Books, New York, 1964, p. 304. At least "seven" in E.R. Chamberlin, *The Bad Popes*, The Dial Press, New York, 1969, p. 174.
22. Dominican friar Savonarola in Friedrich Gontard, *The Chair of Peter*, Holt, Rinehart and Winston, New York, 1964, p. 355.
23. Walter Ullmann, *A Short History of the Papacy in the Middle Ages*, Methuen & Co., London, 1972, p. 319. Also, John, p. 323. Also, Chamberlin, p. 243.
24. J.N.D. Kelly, *The Oxford Dictionary of Popes*, Oxford University Press, Oxford, 1986, p. 119. Also, Gontard, p. 201. Also, Ullmann, p. 113. Also, John, p. 162.
25. **Pope John XII**
Incest and calling on the devil/demons in Gontard, p. 204. Also, Jerrold M. Packard, *Peter's Kingdom*, Charles Scribner & Sons, New York, 1985, p. 243. Also, Chamberlin, p. 43.

Death by an enraged husband in Malachi Martin, *The Decline and Fall of the Roman Church*, G.P. Putnam's Sons, New York, 1981, p. 126. Also, Gontard, p. 207.

Death a week after suffering a stroke while in bed with a married woman in Kelly, p. 127. Similarly, John p. 167.

Nuns and priests marrying

Were nuns and priests to marry, they would raise their children to know Jesus. Over the past centuries, untold numbers of these children would have entered heaven, leading others to glory with them.

To stop this, Satan's plan was to forbid nuns and priests to marry. Popes have carried out the plan diabolically.

26. Roper poll of 3,000 women, released in the spring of 1990. Financed by Philip Morris USA in the name of Virginia Slims.
27. November 1956.
28. August 1968.
29. Matthew 24:30,31.

And he dreamed
that there was a ladder
set up on the earth,
and the top of it
reached to heaven;
and the angels of God
were ascending and
descending on it!
　　—Genesis 28:12
　　　Amplified

The House Painter's Ladder

I'M a painter. A house painter. All day long I go up the ladder, down the ladder. Up the ladder, down the ladder. At night when I'm overtired, I sometimes see houses floating in my sleep. As I toss and turn, the houses toss and turn.

In my dream, the houses are always freshly painted. Fire engine red houses. Lemon yellow houses—with broad strokes of green and pink slashed across them. Light brown houses—with dark brown paint dripping down the final coat. So I toss some more.

No, I'm not a drinking man. I'm a painter. All day up and down, up and down the ladder.

One night . . . I dreamed a different dream. It wasn't really me making up the dream—it came to me, if you know what I mean. I dream houses, but this dream had no houses. Only a ladder. Sort of. Not a wooden ladder, but a ladder made of . . . light. You could see the outline and know it was a ladder, but you could see right through it! I woke up with a start—wide-awake. I knew as well as I know my own name that this was no ordinary dream but a vision. My name? My name is Jacob. [1]

Why God chose to show this ladder to a common house painter, I don't know. I'm a Bible-believer, maybe that's why. I've been asking the Lord to put me on the right path. And I've been asking for power in my life! Maybe that's it. Anyway, I'll share the dream with you.

The dream is about the gifts of the Holy Spirit.[2] Not earthly gifts, mind you—which would be like a wooden ladder. No, the spiritual gifts are special, wonder-working, over-and-above earthly gifts! The nine gifts are power, God's light shining through! The gifts are even in the right order, for as we journey we are being made into the likeness of Christ.

It is the Holy Spirit who operates the gifts for the common good, giving the right gift, at the right moment, with the right amount of power to a servant who has turned in his old wooden ladder for a new ladder of light.

The bottom rung of this spiritual ladder is **speaking in tongues.** Now, hold on! I know many people are turned off by this. It's not for everyone, that's for sure, but it's there for those who want it. Skip it and step to the second rung if you want, but here's the news about it.

Tongues is a prayer language that lifts prayer to the skies. It is a spiritual gift renewing prayer. It is prayer as God hears prayer because it is breathed by the Holy not the human spirit.

Tongues—which is speaking a language not learned with the human mind—is not babbling. It is a recognizable language.[3] It is at the bottom of the list because it gives us a talking acquaintance with the one who shines through all the gifts. Tongues is a gift to the grassroots opening up the avenue to the other gifts. It is a wonderful entry gift. Not the only way to climb to the top, mind you, but for some a beginning step.

Beginning at the bottom in a one to one relationship, we talk to God not with *our* language, but with his. We give God control of our tongue. Our tongue, but God's spirit quickening it.

Wonderful as earthly prayer is, a heavenly language of tongues is even better, for the Holy Spirit is never too weak to pray, knows what to pray for, is able to present the prayer before

God, and prays in harmony with God's will and plan for us.[4] But the gift needs to be kept simple. Doctrines set in cement about "initial sign," "baptism," "permanent, on-going gift," and "Required!" are not helpful. Tongues is a language for talking to God. Simply speak it.

Do all speak in tongues?[5] No. Jesus did not speak in tongues, he *is* tongues! He is the original Word.[6]

Old Testament servants of the Lord were so baptized in the supernatural gifts they put modern, one-gift-speakers-in-tongues to shame. The wisdom of Solomon. The knowledge of Moses. The faith of Noah. The healings and miracles of Elijah. The prophecies of Isaiah. The discernment of Samuel. You can even add the speaking in tongues of Saul. So maybe bottom-rung people shouldn't get too uppity, right?

What was given to these Old Testament men individually was poured out for all who want it at Pentecost. Yet all God's people don't speak in tongues. Why? Well, all paint isn't Sky Blue, but paint is still paint. So let's work together and get on with things.

On the same rung is a companion gift: **interpreting the tongues** being spoken. Why be left in the dark speaking an unknown language? What a joy to hear what the Holy Spirit is speaking on our behalf! Desires too deep to unearth. Thoughts too hidden to search out. Hurts too fearful to look upon. Joys too great to contain! These the Holy Spirit lifts up to the full godhead. Seek the companion gift to know yourself as you are known by God.

An interpretation of a spoken tongue may be given by anyone with the gift so the body of Christ might be built up. The interpreter doesn't know the language any more than the speaker. Word and interpretation are both divinely given. If the language is known—and eye-opening experience for an unbeliever—the listener may simply translate it, for it is a known language.[7]

How do you receive the gifts? Just ask the Giver of good gifts for them.[8] The supernatural gifts may come softly or with a shout of glory. They may come with tears of cleansing or with laughter. They may come when you are alone or in a congregation. In the day or at night. The gift and the manner of coming will often fit your personality. But keep on seeking, for you do not know the Father's time for giving good gifts that are in his will to give to you.

In my dream I saw angels going up and down the ladder—a painter notices things like that. The angels were bringing messages from God and returning with longings too deep for words. Sent with instructions, the angels also returned with responses of persons and nations.

We need to know who these angels are, whether messengers from God or fallen angels slipping into the picture from Satan's kingdom to deceive us.[9] To climb higher toward heaven, we need to learn who's who in the spirit world. Rung number two is **discernment of spirits.**

I remember when I first saw Rachel, the woman I would one day marry. I sensed a lovely spirit in her. How different from the morning I looked into the face of my first wife, Leah. I saw deceit! Oh, how I wish I had discernment earlier!

In my dream of the ladder, God's angels were of light because Christ is the light of the world.[10] Yet God permits Satan's angels to appear to us as light, for, unless we experience them, how are we going to discern them? On earth, deceiving angels sometimes appear through people who say, "Trust me." "I'm your friend." "Peace."

The three spirits—divine, satanic, and human—that move in our world may appear through the same person at different times. A divine spirit inspired Peter when he said, "You are the Christ, the Son of the living God."[11]

A satanic spirit was at work when Peter rebuked Jesus. Jesus had told the disciples the Son of Man must be killed and the third day raised to life. "Never, Lord," insisted Peter. "This shall never happen to you!" Jesus turned and answered Peter, "Out of my sight, Satan! You are a stumbling block to me."[12]

A human spirit was hurt when Peter was asked a third time by Jesus, "Do you love me?" With a grieving, human spirit Peter replied, "Lord, you know everything; you know that I love you."[13]

The best of people are met by all three spirits. The worst of people are met by all three spirits. We need the gift of discernment to know what spirit is working through the people around us—and what spirit is knocking on *our* door!

Many would-be pilgrims climb back down from this rung. It is disillusioning. Having tasted the wonderful sweetness of God, we now get a sour taste from time to time as things we are "told" turn out to be false. We feel deceived—for that is exactly what Satan's fallen angels want. God watches to see if we climb back down and quit, or if we will stay with it. If we accept the mocking defeats, humiliations, disillusionment and confusion—courtesy of Satan's angels of "light"—we will be ready for the next rung.

Prophecy is a message from God.[14] It is God "telling forth" what he wants known about the here and now[15] as well as the future.[16] When the events happen, we come to know the spirit giving us these prophecies is a true spirit. Hearers also come to know the prophet receiving the message is in tune with the right spirit.

I look forward to the times when I can tell my thirteen children what God has for them. It is one of the joys of being a father.

Prophecy may come in the spoken word or a vision. The meaning may be veiled and hidden so people and Satan will keep hands off in trying to change a course that God has chosen.[17] When the event is fulfilled, the veil is lifted. *Then* the meaning seems so simple!

The advantage of God giving a prophecy in a vision, a word-picture, or a dramatic act is that a "picture" saves the prophet trying to remember a thousand words; plus, a picture is graphic, memorable, and may be flashed to mind by God at any time. In addition, pictures have layers of meaning. Some people are happy with the surface meaning; others appreciate the rich character of details and depth. If a prophecy is less than clear, it's because God wants us to keep returning to him for updates.

Visions and word-pictures are the language of the spirit.[19] Our human spirit shouldn't run from these pictures, but should welcome God talking to us in this way. Prophecy can be as simple as the Lord unfolding a picture in our mind's eye that is meant just for us. It may even be a picture of our life's walk. God may even add to the picture as the years go by.

Supernatural and "uncommon" prophecy is given by God. Future predictions are not the result of sweat and long hours searching out the mysteries of the Bible,[20] hoping to figure out with the human mind the date Jesus will return and the date the planet earth will burn up.[21] Poke into the future and you will be answered by false spirits. True prophecy is *given* when God wants a thing to be known.

Where are the prophets of today? Don't look for some bearded guy walking down the street. Look in the mirror.[18] Hey, prophecy isn't just for kings and nations. It's for us little guys, too.

Climbing higher we come to "out-of-the-ordinary" **miracles**. A miracle is the good supernatural entering the natural world and doing a mighty work. I remember once building a fence of poplar wood. Looking at the fence with human eyes, I saw only a wooden fence. It was a barrier to seeing miracles. But looking at the poplar with the eyes of faith, I saw through the fence to the miracle God was working with spotted goats and black sheep.

So many miracles of God—the so many sunsets, births, and changed hearts—are missed by our dull eyes. But yes, pray for a miracle when one is needed. Yes, expect one, for to a God who created the heavens, what's a little miracle on earth? But keep your eyes open, for God works his mighty deeds through the commonplace—like little lambs, goats, and poplar sticks.

Now we are brought a little higher, to the rung of "extra-ordinary" **healings**. At this level we look around and see many people entering our picture. They may be family or strangers. But they are hurting. I've got a thigh out of joint. Also, for many years I had bad memories of a bitter fight with my brother over an inheritance. I was hurting. I needed healing. But different hurts need different healings.

There are gifts (plural) of healings (plural) for the various types of sicknesses.[22] *Spiritual sickness* is caused by sin and cured by saying, "I'm sorry. Forgive me, Lord, for . . ." Then receive his forgiveness and be restored by doing whatever the Lord leads you to do—even if it means hugging your brother. *Emotional sickness* may be caused by being unloved in the past and may be cured by an inner healing. A counselor may help to bring about a healing of both the past memories and present wounds. *Physical sickness* finds its cause in the physical world and may be treated by a medical doctor.

Demonic sickness—which may attack the mind, emotions, spirit, or body—is caused by low order, evil spirits (demons). What is called for is deliverance, the casting out of demons. Who does this? Skip the franchises that put out "Ghostbuster" signs. Like all the gifts, it is not for the titled few, but for the common Christian who wants to do the Master's will and is called to this work.[23] The healing for all the above sicknesses comes from the Great Physician, who heals the whole person.

Divine healing comes directly from God. Faithless people sometimes came to the healing services of Kathryn Kuhlman to mock and ridicule. Surprisingly, *they* were sometimes healed by God! God heals whomever he wants![24]

Faith healing arises from the deposit of faith placed inside a person by God. The big problem here is thinking we are Aladdin and by rubbing our lamp of faith we can command our God/genie, "Heal me! Honor my faith!" Claiming promises in the Bible that are not universal but were meant for someone else at another time and place is foolish . . . probably even arrogant. God will quicken a written promise from the Bible making it a living word for us if he (not we) chooses. On *this* living Word, friends, we can have faith. [25]

If a plan, a healing, or a prophecy originates with God, God will see it through. If the plan, healing or prophecy originates with a human, then the flesh and blood person will have to see it through.

We need to be open to all the gifts and let God decide if and when he will shine through us with any of them. [26] To seek the Giver of the gift, not the gift, is a good thought. With the Giver living in our life, any of the gifts may be awakened at any time.

From the rung of "special" **faith,** our vista widens. We see more lands, more people. We see more needs, but we have stepped into more power. Frankly, an ordinary, daily faith isn't going to make it on this level. [27] What is needed is "wonder-working" faith, and to provide it we need to climb the gateway to heaven through the lower rungs. I'd like to think we can draw near to the heart of God without a climb, but it can't be done. Easy faith, cheap faith, dimestore faith doesn't work.

Remember how Abraham packed up his tent and traveled, not knowing where? Ordinary faith would like a map. Abraham had no map. Moreover, Father Abraham waited 25 years for the son of promise to be born. Ordinary faith would have lasted nine months—no birth, no faith.

Having been tested by faith, we find we *know* and understand God better. The next rung is "singular" **knowledge,** which is information revealed by God. It is not learned through the natural mind.

All the earthly kingdoms of eat and drink have grown distant from this height. It is easier to look ahead to God and his store-house of knowledge than to look back on what is contained in books and floppy disks. How can we trust human knowledge when it changes from day to day? The earth is flat one day, round the next. It is a pleasure to stand on this rung and look ahead to him in whom all knowledge dwells. [28]

What is given to the believer at this level is a *word* of knowledge. A word is not a sentence, not a paragraph, not a book.

Just a word. A fleeting, revealing, "spoken" word. It answers what needs to be known but doesn't give the whole story. The believer needs to keep returning, to keep seeking for we are never given enough to go off on our own.

Neither is a believer given so much that he or she becomes puffed up with conceit. Just a word, a fleeting word. It passes in time. If forgotten, the Holy Spirit will bring it back to mind. But believers are expected to keep God's word in our hearts and to treasure it day and night. Words are not given to be tossed away lightly or be crowded out of a heart that is filled with earthly treasures.

I remember when my son Joseph was born. I *knew* in my heart he was special. And so he was. To me, Joseph was a coat of many colors!

As pilgrims become filled with the knowledge of God, we may then be brought to the rung of "supernatural" **wisdom.** This wisdom is God applying knowledge through us. This wisdom is not from a little earthly mind, but is the splendor of the many-sided wisdom of God, which now is able to shine through a pilgrim. Wisdom is so great, even if you have to wrestle an angel to get it, do it!

Supernatural knowledge and wisdom from God can answer the tough questions, the questions the human mind struggles with:

"Is this a person I should marry?"
"Is this a job I should take?
"Is now the time to change jobs?"
"Is this the community where I should live?"
"Is this a house I should buy?"
"Is this how I should invest my money?"
"Is this the church I should join?"
"Is now the time to have a baby?"
"Is an abortion right for me?"
"Is divorce the answer, or is there another way for me?"

Wisdom is what keeps house painters climbing the right ladder . . . what keeps kings like David and Solomon off "wooden" ladders and climbing ladders of light. Wisdom is what keeps nations in line with God's will.

It is airy at the top of the ladder, and the ladder seems to sway. The vista is grand, but the fall is great. It is best to keep our eyes on the gateway to heaven and not look down.

At every level, Satan's fallen angels are permitted to pester and deceive the believer being filled with the Spirit. This keeps the believer turning to God, the giver of the true gift and the unmasker of the counterfeit. The gifts have no power from God when used apart from him or when used by a believer without love.

Ruled by the *human spirit*, tongues become a noisy gong or a clanging cymbal. Discerning spirits becomes writing people off as lost or of no account. Prophecy becomes bossiness, ordering people about, or pictures of us winning worldly fame and fortune. Miracles become a gimmick. Healings degenerate into "*I* did it!" If healings fail, it is because "*You* lack faith!" Faith becomes dogma, with heretics damned. Knowledge leads to a big head: "So? I have more gifts than you, and I'm on a higher rung!" Wisdom leads to wealthy gurus or tin rulers.

Satan's fallen angels, who fly around the ladder, add their own counterfeits. Ruled by the *evil spirit*, the gifts become unraveled, tinkered with, smashed, or stolen. Tongues—often beautiful, gladsome, or softly whispered—become piercing, wailing, or ungodly moans offered to an unknown god. Counterfeit. Interpretations turn into condemnations. Discernment lets lying spirits fly about freely—a carnival shell game of torment. With great fanfare, prophecy sets us up for a big event to happen—then cruelly laughs when the time passes without the event happening. Prophecy may also picture us in the life script of a loser—or with the power to write the life scripts of others, making them losers.

Miracles by occult spirits dazzle simple believers, leading many to follow false messiahs. Counterfeit healings are temporary. Ridiculing spirits laugh at faith, causing believers to hesitate or abandon their calling. A word of knowledge is added on to, until the meaning is reversed. Wisdom is countered with doubt: "Did God really say that?"

Yet beyond the top of the ladder is the ever-fresh love of God. It is the love of God that spills down the ladder, giving a new paint job inside and out to old, rundown "houses." That's you and me. It's the love of God making us new—washed, primed, and brightened with love! And people notice! Don't think they don't.

The gifts bring us near to the *mind* of God. Love brings us near to the *heart* of God. The gifts are power, but love is the finished job—what being new is all about.

Just then I awoke from my dream. I felt refreshed. Energized! *Terrific!* I sprang from my bed—but stepped on my boot and slipped. Welcome to the world of wooden ladders. Recovering, I found I forgot to wash my painter's pants, so I had to wear a dirty pair. Getting into my van, I realized I left my aluminum ladder at the last house I painted. I felt humbled. It's like I slept with a stone for a pillow.

I guess I got a lot more climbing to do before I get off the bottom rungs. But I'll tell you, I'm putting on my climbing boots. There's a whole world of excitement and miracles out there! And the view from the top . . . IT'S GRAND!

Notes

1. The story of Jacob's life is found in Genesis 25:19 through chapter 50. Jacob's ladder is Genesis 28:10–22. See John 1:51.

2. See 1 Corinthians 12:4–11.
   The in-filling of the Holy Spirit comes in stages
   When God breathed into Adam the breath of life, he breathed into him the Holy Spirit. This brought with it the possibility of the nine gifts of the Spirit—but to a low degree. When Christ is received as Lord, more of the spirit of God enters a person, increasing the potential of the nine gifts. However, it is when the fullness of the Holy Spirit is received that the possibility, the potential, the presence of the nine gifts become prominent and even spectacular. Growing in the Spirit is a process.

3. In New Testament times, languages that were "unknown" to Galileans were current, recognizable languages being spoken in Rome, Judea, Libya, Arabia, and Asia. See Acts 2:6,8,11.

4. Romans 8:26,27.

5. 1 Corinthians 12:27–30.

6. John 1:1.

7. **Speaking in tongues is a real language**
   True-life stories illustrate speaking in tongues is not babble, but is a real language. Yet it is a language neither known nor learned by the speaker.

   In Oregon, a young couple attended a full gospel church. He was in the military and, while stationed in Japan, he met and married a Japanese girl. The young couple returned to America and were managing fine—except the woman flatly refused her husband's Christ and continued clinging to Buddhism.

   > One night, after the evening service, the couple was at the altar, he praying to God through Jesus Christ, and she praying her Buddhist prayers. Next to them was kneeling a middle-aged woman, a housewife from the community. As this woman

began to pray out loud in tongues, suddenly the Japanese bride seized her husband's arm:

"Listen!" she whispered in excitement. "This woman speak to me in Japanese! She say to me: 'You have tried Buddha, and he does you no good; why don't you try Jesus Christ?' She does not speak to me in ordinary Japanese language, she speak temple Japanese, and use my whole Japanese name which no one in this country knows!" It is not surprising that the young lady became a Christian!

> —Dennis and Rita Bennett, *The Holy Spirit and You*, Logos International, Plainfield, NJ, 1971, p. 86.

Similarly, a teen-age girl was praying in a room of the Old Asuza Street Mission when a stranger entered. The girl arose, pointed to the man, and spoke a language she did not know. Shortly afterwards, the man told the congregation:

I am a Jew, and I came to this city to investigate this speaking in tongues. No person in this city knows my first name or my last name, as I am here under an assumed name. No one in this city knows my occupation, or anything about me. I go to hear preachers for the purpose of taking their sermons apart, and using them in lecturing against the Christian religion.

This girl, as I entered the room, started speaking in the Hebrew language. She told me my first name and my last name, and she told me why I was in the city and what my occupation was in life, and then she called upon me to repent. She told me things about my life which it would be impossible for any person in this city to know.

The man, dropping to his knees, cried aloud and prayed as though his heart was breaking.

> —John L. Sherrill, *They Speak With Other Tongues*, Pyramid Publications, New York, 1964, pp. 42–43.

Finally, there is the first-hand account of A. E. Humbard, a country preacher from Arkansas at the beginning of the 1900s.

How the Lord would call me into His ministry when I was uneducated and a very bashful boy, I did not know, for I could not talk plain, having an impediment in my speech.

But call the Lord did, like a fire burning in the bones. Because of his "uneducation and difficulty in speaking," Humbard hoped the Lord would "get someone else and let me off."

> The Lord referred me to Moses, where he said, "Who hath made man's mouth? * * * have not I the Lord? Now, therefore, go, and I will be with thy mouth, and teach thee what thou shalt say" (Exodus 4:11, 12).

While probably still a teen-ager, Humbard's first real chance to preach was sprung upon him. On a Sunday afternoon near a row of trees, he looked out upon a gathering of three or four thousand people. Stage frightened, he got up. Then the Spirit of the Lord burned in his spirit. All his Bible reading and preparation began to "roll out" through his mouth. "I feared no man and preached with holy boldness."

> A miracle happened that day. While I was talking the Holy Spirit began to cause my tongue to speak French, and at the close of the service three thousand people or more were weeping and crying. Scores of French people rushed forward and said, "This man cannot speak good English, but he spoke the French language very plain," and wanted to know if I was French, or knew their language. They said, "Strange things have happened. We heard you speak the wonderful Word of God in our own language and understood it." Upon this many of these French people in that congregation were converted, and many more were converted in hearing about it.

Humbard writes about another occasion, during a Sunday morning service at eleven o'clock:

> While I was yet speaking, an old gentleman jumped up, weeping, and said, "Preacher, are you a German?" I said, "No, sir." He said, "Do you speak the German language?" I said, "No, sir." Upon this he said, "I know you do, and I cannot understand how you found out so many things about me. A few minutes ago you were speaking the German language very plainly and looked right at me and told me my name, how old I was, and all the devilment and meanness that I ever did, and that if I didn't repent of it I was going to be lost. . . ."

Then he came up the aisle, fell on his face before God, weeping, and was gloriously converted.

> —A.E. Humbard, *My Life Story: From the Plowhandle to the Pulpit*, 1945, reissued by his son Rex Humbard in the book *Faith is my Inheritance*, Cathedral of Tomorrow, PO Box 3500, Akron, OH 44310, pp. 12,21,34,97.

8. Ask to receive the spiritual gifts

This is the assurance we have in approaching God: that if we ask anything *according to his will*, he hears us. And if we know that he hears us—whatever we ask—we know that we have what we asked of him.

> —1 John 5:14,15 NIV, emphasis added.

Which of you, if his son asks for bread, will give him a stone? If you, then, though you are evil, know how to give good gifts to your children, how much more will your Father in heaven give good gifts to those who ask him!

> —Matthew 7:9,11 NIV

I tell you the truth, my Father will give whatever you ask in my name. Ask and you will receive, and your joy will be complete.

> —John 16:23b,24b NIV

If you remain in me and my words remain in you, ask whatever you wish, and it will be given you. This is to my Father's glory, that you bear much fruit, showing yourselves to be my disciples.

> —John 15:7,8 NIV, emphasis added.

How to begin speaking in tongues

Someone who already speaks in tongues may help with the mechanics of getting started. First, pray together, with the seeker of the gift repeating a prayer like the following phrase by phrase as the helper leads:

> Dear Jesus. Forgive my sins. Wash me clean. Become the center of my life. Now fill me with the Holy Spirit. Thank you, Lord!

Your helper of faith may "lay hands" (the fingertips of one hand) on your forehead to help release your faith. Your helper will be praying on your behalf, often quietly, often in tongues.

To start your frozen lips moving, say aloud, "The Lord's Prayer" or "The 23rd Psalm" or a favorite verse of Scripture or simply repeat the name "Jesus" over and over again. None of these "how-to" mechanics are necessary, but they have proven helpful to some people.

When you receive the gift of tongues, don't go proclaiming it from the housetops to all you know until you get your feet firmly planted. Read books like *The Holy Spirit and You* by Dennis and Rita Bennett, *They Speak With Other Tongues* by John S. Sherrill, and any books by Donald Gee, such as *Concerning Spiritual Gifts* and *Fruitful or Barren?* (Gospel Publishing House).

9. **What the Bible says about deceiving spirits**

> For such men are false apostles, deceitful workmen, masquerading as apostles of Christ. And no wonder, for Satan himself masquerades as an angel of light.
>
> —2 Corinthians 11:13,14 NIV

> Dear friends, do not believe every spirit, but test the spirits to see whether they are from God, because many false prophets have gone out into the world.
>
> —1 John 4:1 NIV

> So, let two or three prophets speak—those inspired to preach or teach—while the rest pay attention and weigh and discern what is said.
>
> —1 Corinthians 14:29 Amplified

> But test and prove all things [until you can recognize] what is good; [to that] hold fast. Abstain from evil—shrink from it and keep aloof from it—in whatever form or whatever kind it may be.
>
> —1 Thessalonians 5:21,22 Amplified

The Bible gives us guidelines for telling who's who in the spirit world

> "*By their fruit* will you will recognize them. Likewise every good tree bears good fruit, but a bad tree bears bad fruit."

> "Not everyone who says to me, 'Lord, Lord,' will enter the kingdom of heaven, but only he *who does the will of my Father* who is in heaven. Many will say to me on that day, 'Lord,

Lord, did we not prophecy in your name, and in your name drive out demons and perform many miracles?' Then I will tell them plainly, 'I never knew you. Away from me, you evildoers!' "

> —Matthew 7:16a,17,21–23 NIV,
> emphasis added.

They [hearers] received the message with great eagerness and *examined the Scriptures* every day to see if what Paul said was true.

> —Acts 17:11 NIV, emphasis added. See 2 Timothy 3:16.

Every spirit that acknowledges that Jesus Christ has come in the flesh is from God.

> —1 John 4:2 NIV. See verses 1–6.

The Bible tells us the power we have over false spirits

The spirits of prophets are subject to the control of prophets.

> —1 Corinthians 14:32 NIV

Resist the devil, and he will flee from you.

> —James 4:7 NIV

We are not carrying on our warfare according to the flesh and using mere human weapons. For the weapons of our warfare are not physical (weapons of flesh and blood), but they are mighty before God for the overthrow and destruction of strongholds.

> —2 Corinthians 10:3,4 Amplified

Put on God's whole armor—the armor of a heavy-armed soldier, which God supplies—that you may be able successfully to stand up against [all] the strategies and the deceits of the devil.

> —Ephesians 6:11 Amplified. See verses 12–18.

The seventy-two returned with joy and said, "Lord, even the demons submit to us in your name." He replied, "I have given you authority . . . to overcome all the power of the enemy."

> —Luke 10:17,18a,19 NIV

Little children, you are of God—you belong to Him—and have [already] defeated and overcome them [the agents of antichrist], because He Who lives in you is greater (mightier) than he who is in the world.

> —1 John 4:4 Amplified.

> For God has not given us the spirit of fear; but of power and of love and of a sound mind.
>
> —2 Timothy 1:7 new KJV

10. John 8:12
11. Matthew 16:16 NIV.
12. Matthew 16:21–23 NIV.
13. John 21:17 New RSV.
14. Haggai 1:3,13.
15. 2 Samuel 12:7–10. Acts 13:1–3.
16. Acts 11:28 and 21:10–11.
17. **Man "helps" God**
    Abraham "helped" God bring a prophecy to pass by fathering Ishmael, born of an Egyptian slave/concubine. God's promised son, however, was always to be Isaac, born of Abraham's wife. Bad blood has existed ever since between the two families, Arabs and Jews. (Genesis 16)
18. Numbers 11:29.
19. Acts 2:16–18 Amplified.
20. [Yet] first [you must] understand this, that no prophecy of Scripture is [a matter] of any personal or private or special interpretation (loosening, solving). For no prophecy ever originated because some man willed it [to do so]—it never came by human impulse—but as men spoke from God who were borne along (moved and impelled) by the Holy Spirit.

    —2 Peter 1:20–21 Amplified. See Jeremiah 23:15–32.
21. He said to them, It is not for you to become acquainted with and know what time brings—the things and events of time and their definite periods—fixed years and seasons (their critical nick of time), which the Father has appointed (fixed and reserved) by His own choice and authority and personal power.

    —Acts 1:7 Amplified
22. Francis MacNutt, *Healing*, Ave Maria Press, Notre Dame, Indiana, 1974, Chapter 11, "The Four Basic Kinds of Healing," pp. 161–168.
23. An authority on the nature of demons is Lester Sumrall, *Demons: The Answer Book*, Thomas Nelson Publishers, Nashville, 1979.

For more "how-to," see MacNutt, Chapter 15, "Deliverance and Exorcism," pp. 208–231.

24. **God heals whom it pleases him to heal**

> While Jesus was in one of the towns, a man came along who was covered with leprosy. When he saw Jesus, he fell with his face to the ground and begged him, "Lord, if you are willing, you can make me clean."
>
> Jesus reached out his hand and touched the man. "I am willing," he said. "Be clean!" And immediately the leprosy left him.
>
> —Luke 5:12,13 NIV

No, it doesn't please God to heal everyone on this earth: Satan's disciples, backsliders, hypocrites and Pharisees—or even devout persons who will grow more devout without the healing. (2 Corinthians 12:9)

In the Garden, Jesus prayed to the Father: "Yet not my will, but yours be done." (Luke 22:42 NIV) These few words are perhaps the most beautiful prayer in the Bible. For people to end a prayer of healing with them is not lack of faith but is saintly. The words point to the one from whom all blessings flow.

25. Paul Yonggi Cho, *The Fourth Dimension*, Bridge Publishing, South Plainfield, NJ, 1979, Chapter 4, "Rhema," pp. 87–113.

26. 1 Corinthians 12:11. Hebrews 2:4.

27. Healings and miracles which did not work at a lower rung may work at this level:

> Jesus rebuked the demon, and it came out of the boy, and he was healed from that moment.
>
> Then the disciples came to Jesus in private and asked, "Why couldn't we drive it out?"
>
> He replied, "Because you have so little faith. I tell you the truth, if you have faith as small as a mustard seed, you can say to this mountain, 'Move from here to there' and it will move. Nothing will be impossible for you."
>
> —Matthew 17:18–21 NIV

28. Colossians 2:3.

For the sake of Christ,
I am well pleased and take pleasure in
  infirmities,
  insults,
  hardships,
  persecutions,
  perplexities
  and distresses;
for when I am weak (in human strength),
then am I (truly) strong—
  able,
  powerful
in divine strength
      —2 Corinthians 12:10 Amplified

The House Painter's Trials

I PULLED my painter's van up to the Maple's house. Out comes Mrs. Maple, a short woman. "Remember . . ."she reminded me in her high, delicate voice. "Call me 'Bonbon'." I smiled weakly. There she stood—200 pounds of bonbons. "Sure thing, Mrs.— Bonbon. And my name is Jacob."[1]

"How nice. Now I want the house painted a gooey light caramel. Like we talked about," she reminded me brightly. "Make the trim like dark brown chocolate bars!"

"Got it." I began unloading the van. She went in—and peeked through the curtains so she wouldn't miss a thing.

As I put on my painter's cap, my thoughts were still wrestling with the ladder of light image I had dreamed.[2] "Lord," I said softly. "How do I get to the top of your ladder?"

As I set up my ladder, the foot of the ladder slipped off a round rock. I found a new footing. This time the bumpy ground left one side up, the other side down. Just as I was beginning to fume, I caught myself. "The Lord is teaching me something . . ."

My mind went back to my dream about the ladder of light. I focused in on the foot of the ladder in the dream, like I had a close-up picture of it. Then I saw what I was meant to see—the ladder didn't rest on the ground at all. *It arose out of the ground!* My spirit did a happy cart wheel. That's it! That explains what had been bothering me—how the ladder can be the Son of Man![3]

As I opened a can of paint—now christened Gooey Light Caramel—I began to understand better the ladder of light. The Son of Man came down the ladder to be born in Bethlehem. He died on a tree and was buried. Then he rose back up the ladder! That's it! Death and resurrection—there's the power! The power of the gifts comes with the old Adam dying and the new Adam rising in power. It's simple! Except— Who wants to die?

Stirring the paint, I knew the Lord was feeding me thoughts on all the ways of dying to our wants and wishes. Each way is sent by him. Each way gives greater power in the gifts. I asked about the way to power—and I was being shown trials!

I laughed to myself as I thought of Bonbon's sweet, high voice. Kind of like baby talk, wasn't it? It reminded me that **speaking in tongues** was one way to power. Imagine a proud, grown-up person having to talk like a baby. "Da-da-da." Humbling, right? Embarrassing . . . humiliating . . . You've got it. But in our surrender, the spirit of the Lord moves in with *power.* Our unruly tongue is tamed by him. Instead of talking venom, our tongue talks praise and caring.

Carrying a plank on my shoulder to the side of the house, the Lord reminded me of another way of dying in order to live a deeper life. **Take up your cross.** A cross is a burden, a weight. It may be the weight of responsibility on the job or in the home. It may be living with a rebellious teen-ager—like the time my daughter Dinah got in "trouble" by her boyfriend.

I felt the plank dig into my shoulder. Shouldering weights is a cross. When it gets too great, we may come to our senses and say, "Here, Lord. You take it." He does, and we are brought closer to him—and given power to do things mightily, even if quietly. He is our burden-bearer. Our little crosses fit into his big Cross.

Leaning the plank against the house, I checked the ladder again to make sure the footing was firm. I worked the ladder into the ground a little more. Then another image came to mind. "Unless a grain of wheat falls into the earth and dies, it remains alone; but if it dies, it bears much fruit."[4]

I got to thinking about the time Dinah was a little girl and the two of us planted radish seeds. The seed is **buried**. How else can I say it? It's just lowered into the grave and covered. As it dies, that poor little seed breaks a hard husk. Then it has to push up the ground burying it. Then it has to fight the hot sun. Then it fights drowning in too much water, or wilting in too little water. It fights weeds. Next it fights being overcrowded by other radishes. But all the time—it's growing. A miracle! By dying, it lives! It bears the "fruit" of a radish.

I started painting the house gooey caramel. As time passed, I continued wrestling with how dying leads to power. If we can accept the experience of being buried, then the Lord can bring us to life. Maybe it's our career that is being buried. I don't know. It's different with different people. But I do know we get the feeling of being in a grave with dirt being heaped on us. With me, it was a dead marriage, a marriage without love for Leah, my first wife. I wish it had been otherwise, but it wasn't.

As I climbed down the scaffold to finish painting the bottom half of the house, out trotted Bonbon with a question. "Do you like the color I chose?"

"It's . . . Tasteful.

"Oh, good. I'm glad you like it." Back she trotted—to peek again through the curtains.

Time for a drink of water. As I poured the water, another way to power came to mind. The experience of **drowning**, then being brought up again. Have you ever felt you were going under . . . suffocating . . . reaching out for help—and found you were only grabbing more water? I remember when my young son Joseph was missing. I felt pulled under by death. I couldn't breathe.

When I finally let go, stopped struggling, and surrendered, the Lord raised me out of my trouble. I could breathe again! Air. Sunlight. New life! That's the other side of drowning. We're more powerful for going under and coming to our senses. Reaching for the Lord to save us is the answer—no doubt about it.

Lunchtime. I looked at my lunch and the sandwich I had made. Cold cuts from Sunday. No accident here, either. Lamb. I nodded my head. The Lord was getting through to me. Another way to power is what the Lord told his flock: "I am sending you out like **lambs among wolves**."[5] Not a pleasant thought. Not a pleasant experience! It's being chewed out. Worse yet, in front of others. Who needs it?! I take that back—we do.

Maybe it was something we did at work that got the boss's goat. "You idiot! How could you do such a dumb thing?!" Or the time we tried to help a neighbor and it backfired. "Mind your own business—and keep out of ours!"

Know the feeling?

I remember how my boss Laban kept changing my salary and cheating me at every turn. Not pleasant, let me tell you. But if we stand firm in the Lord and don't return kind for kind, being savagely attacked does end—and we walk in a deeper spirit.

At least we have a shepherd watching over us who is in charge at all times. Not to spare us, believe me. But to see us through, to heal us, to lead us back to green pastures and still waters. You can't beat how happy that is! But to get there, lambs may have to face the wolves.

If you haven't guessed, there's a price to pay for the gifts. The price of surrender, of dying to "*my* wants, *my* will, *my* way." Trials are tough.

Being **ignored and unloved** is another way of the old Adam dying to find the love and power of God. My father favored my older brother Esau, who was strong and a hunter. Me? I was the quiet one. Sound familiar?

The **wilderness experience** is being lost and feeling closed in. It's like being in a dark forest and everywhere you look a dark shadow is following you. It's being boxed in. It's being on the run, being pursued.

The trial of **endurance** is to see how long you will hold on to God before quitting. I thought my 20 years with Laban would never end.

Being stoned like the prophets of old is a way to power. All you have to do is take a Biblical stand that is not popular—and duck as the rocks fly!

Some of us are called upon to act as **fools for Christ,** others of us are created to look foolish. "Why have you made me to look this way, Lord?" we ask. Too short. Too tall. Bald. A Pinocchio nose. A hooked nose. A flat nose. Eyes too close. Too far apart. Too slanted. Dumbo ears. Big bosom. No bosom. Wide hips. Knobby knees. Bowlegged. Big feet. WHY, LORD?!!!!! Why did you who formed the Rose of Sharon, form me . . . like THIS?!

Waiting on the Lord is a slow death that raises us to power. Seven years—*seven years!*—I waited to marry my lovely Rachel. Then year . . . after year . . . after year . . . we waited for a child. But do you know—our baby Joseph was worth it!

Being afraid makes us weak so the strength of God can shine through. It may only be mustering up the courage to say, "I'm sorry. Forgive me for . . ." But how hard that is! When I was to meet my brother Esau after our disagreement about the inheritance, I didn't know if he was going to break my neck or not. Scared as I was, I still had to go through with it because it was the right thing to do. Praise God, it turned out with a hug of forgiveness!

Sacrificing in the will of God for yourself, someone in the household of God, or someone outside the kingdom is another way to weakness . . . and power. Perhaps caring for a handicapped child or an aged parent. Perhaps standing by a husband or wife who is adulterous, backsliding, unemployed, alcoholic, addicted, crippled—you name it. I remember when my youngest son Benjamin left home. There was so much danger involved, I thought I'd never see him again. It was like sending him off to be sacrificed.

Sorrow reminds us we are only creatures. Dust to dust. When my beloved Rachel died, the night of my sorrow was long. But do you know, there did come a morning with joy.

The sun was starting to get hot. I finished the side of the house just in time to move to a shady side. The hot sun got me to thinking. Another way to spiritual power is the **fiery furnace,** the furnace of affliction. This trial, too, isn't so hot—excuse the expression. But it does burn away the garbage that's inside us—and there's plenty of that!

The feeling is like a fire burning, humiliating us. We feel on the hot seat. Often it's when we did something we knew or thought might be wrong—and got caught. Found out, guilty—we have to take the punishment. It hurts, it burns, it shames—but unless we get the darkness out of us, how can God's light shine through?

I remember in my younger days when my brother Esau and I bargained his birthright for my lentil stew. I think of another time when I deceived my aging father by putting goatskin on my hands and pretended to be my brother, who had hairy skin. My father then gave me the blessing meant for Esau. Still another time I remember is when my older sons made a bloodthirsty attack on our neighbors, who were living at peace with us. Burning humiliations!

Hmph. All I asked the Lord was how to get a little more miracle power into my life! How to get the spiritual gifts to shine through me more. What the Lord gave was the way of babbling like a baby, being ignored, waiting, enduring, playing the fool for Christ, wandering in a wilderness, being afraid, sorrowing, sacrificing, carrying a cross, drowning, being stoned, being attacked by wolves, burning in a fiery furnace, and being buried! Wow! No wonder so many people back off—and settle for nothing.

Not me! Without power, we walk around defeated, down in the dumps . . . victims. Like it or not, we're in a battle down here. Without God's power, we're losers for sure.

Trials pass.[6] And when they do, we are raised with power to the top of the ladder! We are painted with love! Friends, it is for the sake of our Lord I am able to say,
I am well pleased and take pleasure in
    infirmities,
    insults,
    hardships,
    persecutions,
    perplexities
    and distresses;
for when I am weak in human strength,
then am I truly strong—
    able,
    powerful
in divine strength![7]
Praise God!

"Yoo-hoo! Painter . . . I've changed my mind—caramel is too light." It was Bonbon, waving her hand to stop. "I want you to repaint the whole house. What do you think of fudge brown?"

Notes

1. The story of Jacob's life is found in Genesis 25:19 through chapter 50.
2. Genesis 28:10–22.
3. He then added, "I'll tell you the truth, you shall see heaven open, and the angels of God ascending and descending on the Son of Man."
   —John 1:51 NIV
4. John 12:24 RSV.
5. Luke 10:3 NIV.
6. **Bearing the cross to wear the crown**
   Different images have meaning for different people. Maybe some of these images fit trials you have had:
   A dimly burning wick
   A bruised reed
   Tossed about
   Knocked down
   Shipwrecked
   Being forsaken
   A bitter cup
   Pressure
   Jailed.
   Trials—taken in the right spirit of growing—lead
   to greater knowledge,
   to understand the rule of God,
   to greater power,
   to do the common good,
   to greater character,
   to receive the blessings of heaven.
7. 2 Corinthians 12:10 Amplified

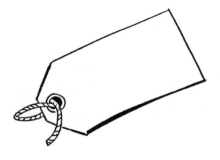

Where you go I will go.
—Ruth 1:16 NIV

Travel Tags

GOD is a masterful travel agent. He has a place for everyone and knows just how much traveling a person needs to do before arriving. God's travel plans are not sight-seeing strolls, but are character-building journeys. Departing a spot that may be a spiritual pigpen, a traveler heads for a destination where there is a robe, a ring, and a fatted calf. In addition, God has a host of lesser agents sent to help others find their way to God's place. The journey is fascinating, the arrival, a homecoming!

> The LORD had said to Abram, "Leave your country, your people and your father's household and go to the land I will show you.
> "I will make you into a great nation and I will bless you."
> So Abram left, as the LORD had told him.[1]

Abraham tagged his possessions for "Shechem . . . Bethel . . . and all points west." The father of our faith set a pattern for all his spiritual children for generations to come.

To Joshua the Lord said:

> "Get ready to cross the Jordan River . . ."

So Joshua ordered the officers of the people: "Go through the camp and tell the people, 'Get your supplies ready. Three days from now you will cross the Jordan here to go in and take possession of the land the LORD your God is giving you for your own.' "[2]

So possessions were tagged, "Jericho: Wall or no wall! . . . Land of milk and honey." God's people are a moving people!

To the Spirit of God who directs us, we need to speak the words of Ruth:

Where you go I will go,
  and where you stay I will stay,
Your people will be my people . . . [3]

Ruth packed her things in Moab and tagged them "Bethlehem." In Bethlehem we find the Savior. In Bethlehem ("house of bread") we find nourishment.

The Lord told Jonah to go eastward to the great city of Nineveh.[4] But Jonah quickly tagged his duffel bags "Tarshish" and quietly slipped aboard a ship going west. God then stirred up a storm at sea that lashed and ripped off the tag. Thrown overboard, Jonah was swallowed up by a great fish that had been tagged "Nineveh" by a Great Fisherman.

Jesus was sending out the seventy two by two to go into every town and place that Jesus himself was to visit. His instructions:

"When you enter a town and are welcomed, eat what is set before you. Heal the sick who are there and tell them, 'The Kingdom of God is near you.' But when you enter a town and are not welcomed, go into its streets and say, 'Even the dust of your town that sticks to our feet we wipe off against you.' "[5]

Their instructions were clear: Carry no purse, bag, or change of sandals. Their travel tags read, "Enter . . . Eat . . . Heal . . .

Tell." If the Welcome Wagon didn't welcome them, the seventy were to move on—on to God's place!

On Easter morning, women went to a tomb to honor Jesus. But angels were posted there with new directions. "Why do you look for the living among the dead? He is not here."[6] Followers of the risen Christ were given tags reading: "Jerusalem . . . Pentecost . . . Clothed with power from on high!"

When Paul preached about the living Lord, many Gentile hearers were glad, but old guard Jews were indignant.

> When the Jews saw the crowds, they were filled with jealousy and talked abusively against what Paul was saying.
>
> Then Paul and Barnabas answered them boldly: "We had to speak the word of God to you first. Since you reject it and do not consider yourselves worthy of eternal life, we now turn to the Gentiles."
>
> The word of the Lord spread through the whole region. But the Jews incited the God-fearing women of high standing and the leading men of the city. They stirred up persecution against Paul and Barnabas, and expelled them from their region. So they shook the dust from their feet in protest against them and went to Iconium. And the disciples were filled with joy and with the Holy Spirit.[7]

When established houses of God don't want to hear about a living, dynamic God who performs miracles, it is time to pack your bags and tag them with the names of new fellowships: "Iconium . . . Lystra . . . Derbe . . . On to Rome!"

Martin Luther, following his trial at Worms, set out for Wittenberg. But God had other plans. Kidnapers—actually friends in disguise—set upon Luther's wagon and whispered in the horse's ear, "Wartburg Castle." Hidden in the castle, Luther would be safe from assassination and safe from being burned at the stake. In the castle, Luther had time to translate the New Testament into German. A valuable change of travel plans, wouldn't you say?

Doors to the Church of England were slammed shut on John Wesley. He received the following note:

> SIR,
> Our minister, having been informed you are beside yourself, does not care that you should preach in any of his churches.

Flabbergasted, Wesley threw up his hands, explaining:

> I simply described the plain, old religion of the Church of England, which is now almost everywhere spoken against, under the new name of Methodism.

Wesley arrived at his home church to face a closed door. Turning a closed door into an open one, he had it announced he would return at six o'clock—to preach standing in the churchyard cemetery!

> I came and found such a congregation as I believe Epworth never saw before. I stood near the east end of the church, upon my father's tombstone, and cried, "The kingdom of heaven is not meat and drink; but righteousness, and peace, and joy in the Holy Ghost."

Not finding the living among the dead churches, Wesley preached in open fields. His travel tickets read "England . . . Wales . . . Ireland . . . America. All the world as my parish!"[8]

At the turn of the 1900s, a Negro preacher attended a new Bible school that believed in Pentecostal power. His name was W. J. Seymour.[9] Invited to preach in Los Angeles, he packed his suitcase and went. There, in a little Negro church, he began to preach about the Holy Ghost.

"Enough!" said the elders afterwards. The next day when the preacher returned, he found the elders had locked the door of the church.

After scratching out that address from the travel tag on his suitcase, Seymour was invited by a sympathetic church member to preach in her old—*really old*—house. As praise swelled and hands clapped and feet stomped, the building shook. And shook. Not able to contain the joy, the dilapidated frame house gave up the ghost. The floor gave way, the walls tumbled, the roof caved in—but no one was hurt.

So much for that address. A new travel tag was written: 312 Azusa Street. As the shouts went up, the rafters shook—but never came down. For 1,000 days the Spirit burned brightly, attracting people from as far as Canada and Great Britain.

What would church leaders do if the Holy Spirit burst on the scene in a respectable mainline church? Let's say an Episcopal church in Van Nuys, California. [10] Perhaps a church pastored by a man educated at the University of Chicago.

It happened, in 1960. Father Dennis Bennett drank the new wine of the Spirit.

"Not in *my* church," thought the bishop of Los Angeles, who banned the activity in his churches. Father Bennett was given a one-way ticket to a far corner of America, the Pacific Northwest.

Officially banned, what would the Holy Spirit do? What *can* he do without a Good Churchkeeping Seal of Approval? The Holy Spirit ignored it. Just as the seal on the tomb was ignored on Easter, so was the Episcopal seal ignored. The flame of the Spirit spread, creating a charismatic renewal!

That brings us to now—and to you. Are you in a dead church? Are you Abram back in the old land of the dead—or are you traveling to a land of promise? Are you Ruth back in Moab—or traveling to Bethlehem? It matters.

When righteous Lot took his family to live in Sodom, he failed to convert Sodom. Not even ten righteous souls could be found. Yet Sodom converted Lot's wife, who looked back to sing "I Left My Heart in Sodom."

The moral is clear: Get out while the getting is good—for if you don't convert Sodom, Sodom will convert you. If you cannot bring life to a dead church, the dead church will suck life out of you and your family. A gathering does not have to be pagan or as wicked as Sodom to kill the soul. A dead church accomplishes the same thing—only slowly.

Feel guilty about leaving? Lot felt bad leaving his sons-in-law in Sodom. His choices? Stay with them and die in the fire—or beg them to come out with him and be free. Taking the hand of an angel, Lot did well to come out.[11]

You should take the hand of an angel and come out of death. Scripture is on your side. Church history is on your side.

If your address reads "Dead church," ask God whether you are to stay.[12] Some churchgoers are meant to be a seed of renewal—actively renewing, not waiting for "something to happen." If you don't feel the Lord leading you to stay, then flee. Is your soul not precious to you? Are the lives of your children not precious to you? Where the Spirit of the Lord is quenched, the soul become chilled . . . the soul dies. Flee!

To where? What do you write on your travel tag? The first step is to survey the land and see what's out there. Your promised land is

> Bible-believing,
> Christ-centered,
> Spirit-filled,
> Servant-called!

It may be a gathering of renewal within a mainline Protestant or Roman Catholic Church. It may be a charismatic or Pentecostal fellowship. There may be folded hands or handclapping, a quiet move of the Spirit or dancing in the Spirit. But there will be a dying to the lust of the flesh, the lust of the eyes, and the boastful pride of life.[13] In their place will be living with the risen Lord.

Use your spiritual *eyes*, the leading of your *heart*, and a clear and quiet *mind* stayed on Jesus that will speak to your soul. Jesus may also send a trusted, mature, and spiritual Christian your way to speak the name of a fellowship. But know this: a parked car isn't going to get you there. "Keep on seeking and you will find."[14]

Once inside, what do you look for? Look for a preacher who preaches from the **Bible.** Don't return if he says, "This Bible story is a myth, but we can learn from it." Listen on if he says, "The Bible is the history of God seeking man."

Look for a preacher who is not ashamed to speak the name "**Jesus.**" Don't return if he lifts up "The church! The church!"— meaning in his mind: the Organization. Listen on if he preaches, "The Cross! The Cross!"

Look for a preacher who is being **filled with the Spirit.** Don't return if the preacher says, "You received all the Holy Spirit there is when you were saved. There is no more." That preacher has stopped growing. Listen on if he cries out, "More, Lord! Pour more of your Spirit into me!" The riches of Christ are unending. The infilling of the Spirit is to overflowing.

Look for the **fruit** on a particular church tree. Dried prunes? Bitter, green apples? Sour grapes? A hard nut to crack? Move on. Stop at the tree that bears love, joy, peace, patience, and kindness. Take a bite and live!

Look at the pews. Are they filled with church potatoes— lumpy Christians who do nothing? Are the pews filled with parents who drop off their children in Sunday School, then go to the sanctuary for an hour of peace and quiet? Find a church of **servants** who come to the Lord of Harvest wanting to be placed in his hands and wanting to be scattered like seeds into the fields of work and home.

Having moved from a dead church to one tagged "Bible-believing . . . Christ-centered . . . Spirit-filled . . . Servant-called!" know when to stop. No home is perfect. Remember to speak the words of Ruth to the Finisher of our faith:

> Where you stay I will stay.
> Your people will be my people. [15]

Then rip off all your travel tags and unpack. You're home.

Notes

1. Genesis 12:1,2a,4a, NIV
2. Joshua 1:2,10,11 NIV.
3. Ruth 1:16 NIV.
4. Jonah 1:2 NIV.
5. Luke 10:8–11 NIV.
6. Luke 24:5,6 NIV.
7. Acts 13:45,46,49–52 NIV.
8. *The Journal of John Wesley,* Moody Press, Chicago, pp. 69,80,98–99,74.
9. John L. Sherrill, *They Speak With Other Tongues,* Pyramid Publications, New York, 1964, pp. 41–43.
10. Sherrill, pp. 61–62.
11. Genesis 18:16–19:26.
12. **Come alive**
    Paul writes:
    > Every one should remain after God calls him in the station or condition of life in which the summons found him.
    > —1 Corinthians 7:20 Amplified

    It is a mistake to interpret these words as meaning:
    > Stay spiritually dead.

    Paul never told people:
    > Stay in Judaism. Do not follow the Way, the teachings of Jesus. Go back to the law of Moses and be circumcised.

    Paul indentified our state or situation as social, racial or externally religious—not spiritual. He wanted people to be content in all stages of life. On the other hand, if an opportunity should come along to better our earthly lot, take it, advised Paul. (Verse 21)

    It may be that the various states in which God *found* us—sinful, slave, poor, sickly, unmarried—may *not* be the state to which God is *calling* us:
    > I pray that you may prosper in all things and be in health, just as your soul prospers.
    > —3 John vs. 2, New KJV

I came that they may have and enjoy life, and have it in abundance—to the full, till it overflows.
—John 10:10b Amplified

Time to move on

Jesus said:

My prayer is not that you take them out of the world but that you protect them from the evil one.
—John 17:15 NIV

It is a mistake to interpret these words as meaning:

Leave the saints in dead churches.

The "world" here means a setting: neighborhood, market place, the planet earth. As for going back to an old place, remember when Jesus received the fullness of the Holy Spirit? He did not return to the carpenter shop.

13. 1 John 2:16 NAS.
14. Matthew 7:7.
15. Ruth 1:16 NIV.

Giving Thanks

THANK you, Sherwood Wirt,
   for founding the Christian Writers' Guild of San Diego.

Thank you, Grossmont Critique Group,
   for speaking faithfully about the manuscripts you read.

Thank you, Author of authors,
   for writing your words on the tablet of my heart.

—Spring, 1994

Index